John S. Cheetham

grow up!

How to raise an adult
by being one yourself

WILKINSfarago

This fully revised edition published 2008
First edition published in 2001 by
Wilkins Farago Pty Ltd
(ABN 14 081 592 770)
PO Box 78, Albert Park, Victoria 3206, Australia
www.wilkinsfarago.com.au

ISBN 978 09804165 1 0 (book)
ISBN 978 09804165 2 7 (e-book)

Illustrations by Phil Scamp (www.layer14.com.au)
Cover/title design by Silvana Paolini
Internal design by Pages in Action
Editing by Andy Whyte Media Services (awms@optusnet.com.au)
Printed in Australia by Griffin Press
Distributed by Tower Books (Australia) and Addenda (New Zealand)

Contents

Young—Creating Reasonable Boundaries—Logical Outcomes or Consequences Are Useful—Teaching Decision-Making Takes Time

5 The Strength to Watch Them Fail

The Problem with Being a Rescuer—Controlling Our Egos—Adults Visualise a Positive Outcome—It's Their Life, Not Ours—Education Is Our Children's Business—Learning Difficulties—Reality's Okay—Are You a Robber?—Communication: Keeping It Simple—Taking the Time—Choose Your Moment—To Nag or Not to Nag?—Is It Worth Saying?—A Family Conference—*Violence and Its Reduction Through a Family Conference*—Focus On the Good Behaviour—Put In the Positives—Speaking for the Child—Sibling Fights—*Dealing Effectively with Sibling Fights*

6 What Is a Normal Teenager?

Going Through Stages—*Early Adolescence*—*Middle Adolescence*—*Late Adolescence*—Iceberg or Volcano?—Teenagers and Study—A Chemical Cocktail—Volcano or Iceberg Parents—Teenage Parties—What About More Serious Behaviours?—Keeping the Door Open—Communication Is the Key—Keeping Negative Emotions Under Control—Recognise the Child's Expression of Feelings—Remind Yourself that You Are the Adult—Hyperactive Kids—Teaching Values and Beliefs

7 Working As a Team

How Flexible Can You Be?—Forgiveness for Errors—Revisit Your Definition of Love—Expressing Love—Managing Emotion—Choosing Our Words—Words Can Energise

8 Conclusion

Self-assessment: Are You On the Right Track?—Self-assessment: Feedback—Postscript—Where Can I Get Help?

Bibliography

Acknowledgements

I pay tribute to all those who have influenced the ideas that form this book:

My daughters, Sarah and Natalie, who fine-tuned my parenting skills and have given me fearless feedback on my performance as a father. The infinite wisdom, practicality and influence of their mother, Bobbie, whose pragmatism and love shines out.

My parents, who didn't quite get the formula right, yet inspired me to study psychology. Emeritus Professor Maurie Balson, who taught me so much, and continues in my life as a mentor and friend.

I also pay tribute to my colleagues: consulting psychologists Chris Pearson, Jason Hine and Angela Gent for their critiques of my ideas. Oh, to be exposed to the merciless barbs of colleagues! I have learned much from Sandy in her effective management of four teenage children as a single parent. Bless them!

The late Michael Tovey, whose insights and expertise in training and personal experiences helped shape the first edition of this book.

Finally, Andrew Wilkins of publishers Wilkins Farago, for his enthusiasm and tolerance and love of cappuccinos, Andy Whyte for his editorial skills, and my colleague Jenni Murray for her infinite patience as I fine-tuned the manuscript.

 Disclaimer: The case studies in this work are based loosely on clinical experience, not necessarily that of the author, and bear little or any resemblance to actual case studies of the author.

About the author

Pyschologist John Cheetham is the founder of the Student Achievement Centre (www.studentachievement.com.au) in Melbourne, Australia, and is the author of the bestselling *Teach Your Child to Spell*. He has over 35 years' experience helping parents and kids, and appears regularly on radio and television around Australia. He conducts regular workshops for parents both in Australia and internationally. In 2006, he was the keynote speaker at the National Parenting Conference in Singapore.

Chapter

Introduction

Do you wish your children would grow up? Is your home a battleground? Do you guide your children or control them? Do you yell at your teenagers and behave like a drill sergeant? This book suggests actions and techniques that you can take to develop responsible behaviours in children from the age of five. They work.

This book is not a recipe for bringing up perfect children. It is a roadmap to bringing up healthy, positive, responsible and achieving children. Do you want to bring up your child to be a well-balanced, fulfilled young adult? In achieving this goal, do you want to reduce the stress and strain of parenting? If so, this book is for you.

Self-assessment: Are You on the Right Track?

Simply respond with a 'yes' or 'no' to each of the following statements:

1   I feel that my life stopped when I had children.

2   I dream of my children leaving home and leaving me in peace.

3   The demands on me never seem to end.

4   Sometimes I wish I was deaf and didn't have to listen to all the yelling and arguing.

5   I never thought I'd end up being a slave.

6   I've become a spy and go through my children's belongings, looking for clues as to what they are doing.

7   'No' has become my most frequently used word.

8   I am a taxi driver to my children.

9   Sometimes I drive around the block instead of going home.

10 I have had a MP3 player installed in the toilet.

If you answered 'yes' to some of these questions, then read on. This book will show you how to teach a child to be responsible in a range of areas: attention to homework and study, financial management and social life. This book will challenge you to create a healthy lifestyle for you and your child.

Although few parents would admit it to others, most are fearful of how society may influence their children. Every child flirts with bad behaviour, but what does a parent do if the flirtation becomes more permanent?

Most parents are fearful that their children will mix with the wrong group, take drugs, drop out of school, be involved in antisocial behaviour, be sexually promiscuous or get into trouble with alcohol or the law.

A choice of school is often made in an attempt to reduce these risks. Such fears can lead to large sums of money being spent on school fees in the hope that the right environment will help to prevent a child from engaging in undesirable behaviour. Sometimes the investment pays. Sometimes it doesn't.

Whatever else you do, it is the relationship that your children have with you that will be the biggest influence on how they turn out.

This book is based on my thirty-five years of experience as an educator and psychologist working with young people and their families. I believe it to be provocative, yet practical and down-to-earth. I have prepared the book as a source of inspiration and as a confidence booster for parents. My perceptions about parenting have also been influenced by my observation of children and adolescents, and my listening to what they say and how they feel about their parents and other adults in their lives. Young people can be very insightful into parental behaviours!

This book respects each parent as a unique adult with their own values and personal history. It acknowledges the differences between individuals, and explains how you can use these to develop better relationships with your children. As your relationship with your children improves, so too will your quality of life.

Every parent is able to quickly learn the skills they need to develop their child into a responsible, healthy and achieving adult. Knowing how to bring up your child to be an independent thinker, capable of making choices and identifying consequences, will bring positive benefits to everyone. Your child will become a strong and responsible adult. You can expect to reduce your fatigue and enjoy your role as a parent. It is a win–win situation.

Irrespective of your own experience, you can be a powerful teacher for your child. Remember:

Adults are the guardians of reality.

Who Taught You the Job?

Let's face it, parenting is a challenge! We are well educated for many of the roles we fulfil in our society. At school, we are trained in leadership, knowledge and social skills, and we are trained for work. Parenting, however, is one role for which there is little training. Flying by the seat of our pants, most of us hope that all will work out through trial and error.

Our own parents have set the base for our parenting techniques. We can observe what other parents do and hope that we get the formula right. Our personality governs how we relate to others, including children. It is the mix of our own personality traits, personal history and observation of others that creates the foundation for our parenting role.

The trigger for the parent role is pregnancy. According to the most recent statistics, Australians produce a new baby once every one minute and fifty-nine seconds, while Americans produce one every eight seconds! The transition from adult to parent could therefore be said to start with an orgasm. For many of us, though, it will signal the start of a lifestyle in which we get less sleep, more worries and a lot fewer orgasms!

A Double-edged Sword

The word 'parent' creates a range of reactions in people. For young people yet to have a family, there is usually eager expectation. For those with a young baby or child, there is often a mixture of joy, fear and fatigue. There are fleeting moments of joy when the child does something for the first time and we bask in its need for love and affection. The child feeds our need to be needed. A baby or young child smiles at us and wants to be cuddled, which makes us feel good and worthwhile as a person.

However, we soon learn that children can be experts in draining us of energy and putting dints in our self-confidence. We can soon lose our sense of wellbeing.

The birth of a child has a significant impact. The adult lifestyle changes to a parent lifestyle. The marital relationship is affected. Sexual relationships and levels of affection between adults change. There is less time to pursue outside interests. Social life often decreases and stress increases. Tiredness and an increasing lack of confidence in the new role of parent result in a permanent change to our sense of self as an adult.

What's the World Going to Do to My Baby?

Parents feel a wisp of fear as their child sets off to school. The child is about to be exposed to the outside world and its influences. If this has already happened to your child, you may remember feeling vulnerable as your total control was lost.

Whether you ever really had complete control is debatable. One thing's certain: from now on other people and influences will play a role in your child's life. They may be exposed to attitudes and values with which you may not agree. This is positive, although rarely perceived as such by parents. Children will grow and be extended in their thinking through this exposure. They will be equipped to live in the external world beyond the family through the feedback they receive about themselves from others.

So many questions go through parents' minds:

- Will they learn easily?
- Will they have an encouraging teacher?
- Will they enjoy school and grow in confidence in their ability?
- Will they be safe?

At primary or elementary school, many issues can arise. The child is exposed to the challenge of formal learning. Some parents expect their child to follow a pre-ordained path. They compare their child to others. Yet the individual differences between children and their learning styles emerge. Each child grows physically, mentally and emotionally at a different rate. This is particularly noticeable in the first three years of school.

CASE STUDY: It's not a race

Janice was very concerned about her five-year-old son Andrew. He had started school and Janice became very actively involved as a parent helper. She would attend the school twice a week to assist with the reading program. Each child in the class was given the opportunity to read a reader to a parent. Completion of a reader led to the book being logged into the child's reading record and a new book selected. It was soon obvious to Janice that Andrew was not making much progress with his reading. She became worried and insisted that Andrew do extra reading at home each night. Andrew objected and started to become defiant. After seeking professional help, Janice learned about individual differences and took the pressure off Andrew. Instead of insisting that he read each night, she implemented a cuddle and story time, where she or her husband read a story to him each night before bed. Andrew responded well to the positive experience, lessened his resistance to reading and by Grade 3, with normal teaching, he was one of the best readers in his group.

Janice, like many parents, experienced the anxiety of feeling helpless. She learned, however, that by:

- not expecting too much too soon, and
- building a positive emotional connection between reading and her child, positive gains could be made.

It is important to recognise that children mature at different rates, and that comparing your child with others, particularly in the first three years of school, is unhelpful.

Should Andrew not have made progress with his reading, the next step would have been to seek professional help from a psychologist to assess Andrew's learning style.

Secondary Education

As elementary or primary school days end and children begin secondary education, parental concerns intensify:

- Will they get through puberty?
- Will they be able to cope with different teachers and subjects?
- Will they do well enough at school to be employed?
- Will they cope with peer-group pressure?
- Will they be the victims of bullying?
- How will they handle their sexual development?
- Will they experiment with alcohol and drugs?

The individual differences in development continue throughout secondary school and into early adulthood. The secondary-school child has to be more organised to cope with the change of teachers and the variety of subjects and their demands. Puberty is well under way or about to begin: the age of innocence is over. Mood changes become more frequent and a previously loving and respectful child may view their parents with increasing cynicism and even loathing. They love and hate their parents simultaneously. Adolescents, free of the adult responsibilities to come, have the time to develop and nurture friendships. Parents soon see that their children's friends' ideas and thoughts are infinitely more important to them than those held by parents. Adolescents seem to be less willing to engage with their parents or to listen to their points of view. They challenge most things a parent says. This is not unusual. It is a key step on the way to adulthood.

Going Their Own Way

As children grow and mature, their ability to assess their world increases (assuming that they have no intellectual deficit). They become aware that there are ways of living life and doing things that differ to their parents' way of living. No longer do they innocently accept that their parents are 'perfect'.

Education assists this process. Adolescents cease to see the world in the simple way of a child. They are taught to think, to analyse and to challenge what they see and experience. As parents are part of their world, they also will be exposed to the questioning mind of the young person. As parents, we can't escape this scrutiny: our very ability to address our children's concerns is being brought into question. We will be under the microscope.

The Exasperating Teenager

Your adolescent's experimentation with friendships, ideas, feelings and social issues can be exasperating. Yet this willingness to explore the world and themselves will help determine the life they lead as an adult. If earlier we were feeling a little unsure about our ability as a parent, we are now sorely tested!

During this phase, the idea of a happy home can become a distant memory. Simple things can develop complexity. Keeping a room clean, helping with household chores, being polite – all seem to become impossible challenges. Everything is questioned or ignored by the adolescent. Harmony within the family can quickly disappear. This can be very tiring for parents, but the good news is that you don't have to live in exhaustion for the next decade. You can have more control.

CASE STUDY: The house of doom.

Visiting the Edmonds' home was like stepping into a funeral parlour. The house was tastefully decorated, but the atmosphere was one of stony coldness. The counsellor had visited with them in an attempt to get the family talking with each other in a relaxed manner. The silence that she encountered was the usual shutdown following the shouting and arguments that took place nightly.

Mrs Edmonds complained that it didn't matter what she said, someone would always take offence at it. 'They would argue that black was white and white was black', she said. Mr Edmonds avoided coming home until as late as possible, in the hope that most of the children would have gone to bed. Their children, aged 8, 10, 15 and 17, were experts in irritating their mother and each other. The 17-year-old boy targeted his 15-year-old sister's acne, the 8-year-old teased the 10-year-old for being overweight and ugly. The 15-year-old hit the 8-year-old, as a preventative measure, in case he looked like coming anywhere near her bedroom. In general, they seemed like a typical family, the counsellor mused to herself, as Mrs Edmonds mixed the preparation of a cup of coffee for her with threats of death directed toward the 17-year-old.

'Why did I have children?' Like Mrs Edmonds, many parents have asked this question, as they reflect on the nightmare of their existence with their teenagers. It certainly can prematurely age a parent!

As you read this book, reflect on the role of a parent and the skills of parenting. Examine what I suggest in relation to your own experience and observations as a parent. Be open-minded enough to be challenged by what you read. Through this process, a clearer perception will emerge of the choices you can make – to the benefit of your child, for your own sanity and for the creation of a happier family life.

Chapter 2

Stop Acting As a Parent – Be an Adult

A Roadmap For Life

The purpose of this book is to suggest that you can play a very effective role in assisting your children to develop the skills they need for a healthy and productive life. To do this, you do not have to trade in or compromise your own set of values. We are all individuals after all. Life experience has given us a set of values that is an important guide to what we believe and how we behave. Values and beliefs are like a roadmap for life. They guide us in what we do and how we do it. Our culture, religion or spiritual beliefs, our education and our own families in which we grew up, all contribute to this roadmap.

Can you imagine enjoying your children growing up? Mrs Edmonds couldn't! Like many parents, she believed that the best way to bring up a child is to tell them what to do. I aim to challenge some of these common ideas and beliefs about parenting.

Stop Being A Parent

As an adult, once we accept the label 'parent', it changes the way in which we see the world and behave. The word 'parent' brings with it strong feelings of responsibility, challenge and pressure. Left unchallenged, these feelings can create thoughts and habits that can be counter-productive.

As a key for something more positive to happen, I am going to ask you to consider the idea that you could stop acting as a parent. 'How absurd!' is probably your immediate response. I'm not suggesting that you give your children away (although there are some good boarding schools!). Nor am I suggesting that you run away from home, however attractive that fantasy might seem.

What I am doing is inviting you to keep an open mind. Think about the ideas that I am going to share and, at the end of our time together, make up your own mind about how you are going to fulfil your role with your children. Remember: you create the recipe that will work for you. All I can do is make a suggestion as to some of the ingredients that you might like to use.

Take A Fresh Look

It is a pretty safe bet that what is happening in your family at the moment isn't getting you the results you want, and that is a motivation for your reading this book. Alternatively, you might be losing confidence or seeking clearer directions. Either way, I invite you to read on. Your reward will be a clearer and more positive approach to the task of parenting. This will result in less stress and anguish. A happier home is achievable!

There is an old maxim:

**If doing what you are doing doesn't work,
then it's time to do something differently.**

CASE STUDY: A fresh approach to an old problem

Twenty-year-old Tony's job was to deliver and install large bottles of gas to homes in a rural area. He would manually load his utility, drive to a home, roll the bottles off the utility and drag them to the spot where they were to be installed. It was hard, physically demanding and cumbersome work. It didn't matter how efficient Tony was in his work, it was slow and time-consuming because of the awkward nature and weight of the bottles. One night, in bed, he thought about how he did his job and how he might be able to reduce the physical demand. In his mind, he created a large wheeled trolley with the capacity to negotiate areas other than pathways. He sketched his design and set about manufacturing a prototype. It worked. The new trolley enabled him to achieve his goal of less physical strain.

Tony was as committed to his job as he had always been. The creation of a new trolley helped him improve his quality of life. It would have been stupid for him to continue to do the job in the same way, when he knew that what he was doing wasn't working very effectively. All it took was the ability to challenge what he was doing and to seek a different way of doing it. Tony went through a number of steps:

- recognising that he was unhappy with the way things were
- desiring to see an improvement
- analysing the problem
- creating other options or solutions
- deciding to do things differently.

All the skills Tony needed to do this were likely to have been influenced by good parenting and education.

But What Can I Do, Apart From What I'm Already Doing?

Like most parents you may have tried different things with your children, yet feel as though you've gone around in circles. You may have observed other parents and their children. You have probably picked up ideas here and there and, like Tony in our example above, created your own ideas. There is bound to be value in many of these ideas, but we are often too impatient – if a problem can't be fixed or an improvement gained immediately, we tend to change direction too soon. Whatever you may to choose to do, think about the first concept that I am going to share with you:

Change your thinking as a parent.

What's wrong with the word 'parent'? Like the words 'cancer' and 'dyslexia', it triggers strong and often negative emotions. The word 'parent' brings back childhood memories of our own parents, and we recall the power they had over us.

Of course, being a parent itself isn't bad! But all the attachments that now come with the word make it a hindrance rather than a help. Consider some of the things that the word 'parent' brings to mind:

- memories of your own childhood and how your parents treated you
- illusions of power and authority over children
- blind obedience from your child
- gratitude from your child for what you do
- the need to protect your child from outside influences
- the automatic right to be in control – you brought them into the world, after all!
- the view that children can't think until they get older and therefore need to be told how to do things.

Where Do We Learn To Be Parents?

The answer is, in part, from the example of the adults who brought us up. They may well have been good parents, and we may look back with affection and respect for what they did and how they did it. On the other hand, we may be very aware of the deficiencies in parenting that we were subjected to. Our experiences as children will, to some degree, shape our style of parenting with our own children. One thing we probably all have in common when we think of our parents is that they had power!

The difficulty that arises in transferring a parenting style from one generation to another is that society changes. The parenting techniques used by your parents may not be appropriate to your children. Times change! But values don't necessarily need to change. The love and affection that hopefully was shown to you can still be shown to your child. A parent's cuddle, warmth and unconditional love is precious. Techniques, however, do need to be appropriate to the society in which you and your child now live.

These days children are encouraged to think, analyse, debate and discuss ideas from a very early age. They are not passive recipients of other people's ideas. As a society, we will not respond effectively to the needs of the next generation unless we consciously engage ourselves in their upbringing. Taking a role as a parent without clear and conscious thought incurs the risk of adopting techniques that are born of habit and lack of thought. There is a strong need for us to consciously assess our role and the techniques that we choose to use. Failure to do this analysis results in parents slipping into patterns of behaviour that can create problems. A common problem is the adult who unthinkingly takes on the parenting style that is characterised by:

- telling the child what to do
- fear of the child expressing an opinion
- fear of the child making a decision
- failing to teach the child reasons for actions
- not respecting the child's intelligence
- seeing the child as automatically 'bad' or 'naughty' and therefore requiring constant parental intervention and supervision.

If you try and deal with children with a parent's hat on, you are in trouble. I invite you to think about acting differently. This book will show you how.

The 'Over-parent' Danger

Achieving a balanced approach as a parent is very difficult. This constitutes another danger arising from constant use of the parent hat. There is a group of parents who embrace the parenting role with such passion that they completely lose their objectivity.

An 'over-parent' takes full responsibility for the child and everything that the child does. Over-parents are smotherers. They choke the child's development. Adoptive parents, parents of only children and parents of sick or chronically ill children can be prone to over-parenting.

Characteristics of over-parenting are:
- believing that all decisions must be made by them, as children are too immature to do so
- intruding into every petty detail of their children's lives
- constantly asking their children questions
- always giving their opinion on every aspect of what the child is doing and who they mix with
- being strongly motivated to protect the child – 'We are only doing this for your own good.'
- over-reacting to minor occurrences
- maintaining inflexible routines
- taking life too seriously
- believing in power and total control
- feeling weighed down with the 'burden of responsibility' of being a parent
- imposing very high expectations – asking 'Why did you not get 100 per cent?' even if the child got 98 per cent in a test at school
- emphasising achievement over effort.

Characteristics of the over-parented child include:
- being fearful or unsure about their own decisions
- reluctance to make decisions
- lacking personal confidence
- anxiety about disapproval from adults and peers
- problems in dealing assertively with authority
- being awkward at times in their relationships with peers
- reluctance to take positive risks
- rebelliousness in adolescence
- a tendency not to achieve for themselves and therefore to be perceived by others as lacking motivation
- engaging in deception with their parents in a struggle for independence
- being high achievers and often 'pleasers'
- perceiving themselves as 'not good enough'
- being a perfectionist.

When you look at the behaviours commonly displayed by over-parented children, they are unlikely to be those behaviours you'll hope your own children acquire. I will come back to this issue in Chapter XX.

CASE STUDY: I can't breathe

Jenny was the eldest in her family. Her mother, a feminist, always had great dreams for Jenny. From an early age Jenny's mother took great pains to ensure that Jenny was not going to suffer the oppression she had experienced in her own family about the woman's destiny of being a wife and mother.

Each day after school, Jenny's mother would ask questions about her homework. She would regularly contact the school to check with the teacher that Jenny was 'up to date'. Jenny's mother would be very sad if she received anything less than an A for her work. Over the years of her secondary education, Jenny became anxious and unsure about herself.

Jenny's mother also wanted to make sure Jenny associated with the 'right' people. She would not allow Jenny to socialise with certain other class members who she saw as 'bad influences'. When Jenny was invited to teenage parties of people who her mother 'disapproved of', her mother banned her from attending. On the rare occasion that she allowed Jenny to go, she would be rigidly inflexible about the time at which she had to come home. Things were never discussed or negotiated. Jenny was told by her mother what was appropriate and what was inappropriate.

Jenny became angry about her mother having so much control over her life and began to become deceptive, sneaking out to parties behind her mother's back. At school, most of Jenny's friends would tease her for being a 'mummy's girl'.

Having had most of her decisions throughout her life made for her by her mother, and carrying a well-justified anger, Jenny attended a party where she got very drunk. She did not come home until late the next day and did not remember what had happened. Her mother was horrified and angry. Jenny felt guilty because she had not met with her mother's approval, but was still angry about the control her mother was having over her. The episode was so horrifying that her mother in desperation took Jenny to a psychiatrist to have her treated for her behaviour problem.

Over time, Jenny became so torn inside she began to stop eating to gain some control over her life (in her mind). Jenny became so ill that she ended up in hospital. This confirmed for her mother how important it was for her to be in control of Jenny's life because Jenny was obviously unable to be responsible. 'She was the same at school,' her mother said. 'I would always have to make sure she did her work.'

The 'Under-parent' Danger

Some parents have little involvement with their children. They pursue their own lifestyle as a priority and the children are expected to fit in. 'Under-parents' are usually egocentric. These parents lack the ability to give appropriate warmth and encouragement to the child. Their own needs and happiness are more important than their commitment to their child. Almost universally they would deny this to be true. They are so self-centred that they are blind to others' needs. This can often be observed in parents who are separated or divorced.

Characteristics of under-parents are:
- reluctance to become positively involved in their children's lives
- seeming, on the surface, to do the necessary things for the child
- spending little time genuinely involving themselves in their children's lives
- dropping children at a sporting function but not watching them play
- failing to set clear boundaries for children
- failing to ensure that children carry through with their commitments
- treating children as friends or equals, as opposed to children who need guidance and boundaries.
- being unsupportive or uncooperative with the other parent in bringing up the children
- spending a lot of time convincing others about how committed they are as parents

Characteristics of 'under-parented' children include:
- inability to plan or set goals
- living 'in the now'
- starting things but not finishing them
- having a *laissez-faire* (permissive) view of life
- lacking a long-term vision of their future
- taking risks and having a poor understanding of the implications of their actions (e.g. drug-taking)
- being disorganised
- low sense of identity (because they have lacked boundaries)
- resenting all reasonable parental discipline
- developing anti-authoritarian views.

Often under-parented children become adults who lack vision, direction and control over their lives.

CASE STUDY: I need a job now

John was a young man whose parents had always been open to him doing his own thing. When John started to fail because he was not handing in his homework, his parents said to him that he should change subjects because the ones he had been doing were 'not his thing'. John did so, and continued a lifestyle of partying and sleeping at his girlfriend's place for at least half the nights of the year. His homework and study patterns throughout the year were erratic.

In December of his final year of secondary education, John was sick of his girlfriend and decided it was time to move on. Surprisingly, he passed his assessments with very low results.

Over the Christmas break, he attended a lot of parties and became quite involved with a group of people who were into various drugs and partying. Within this group, he found a new girlfriend and they shared a few months of a very chaotic relationship together. She became pregnant and decided she would go through with the pregnancy. John was faced with fatherhood and 'partnerhood', although he didn't really want to spend his life with her.

John thought he had better do something about getting a job to support his 'family' but didn't know where to start. In exploring career options, John seemed very remorseful that he couldn't go on to university with his mates. His parent's reactions to his situation were very calm and they presented as being almost disinterested. His father coldly lectured him and his mother seemed quite confused in her view of what was occurring.

Neither the authoritative (over-parenting) nor the permissive (under-parenting) techniques were helpful in enabling Jenny and John to make effective decisions and be responsible for their own lives. Jenny had been so dominated by her mother that she was smothered and unable to grow as a person. John was so lacking in emotional support and positive guidance that he was isolated and ineffective in taking control of his life.

Parenting *is* problematic, but many of the difficulties can be avoided by changing our thinking about our techniques.

Are You A Parent – Or An Adult?

Have you noticed that once people become parents, their view of themselves changes and they stop being adults in their relationship with their children?

CASE STUDY: Over the limit

Paul was the managing director of a large corporation, responsible for a multi-million dollar operation. He was well respected by his co-workers and employees and had developed a reputation for his practical and down-to-earth approach to issues. He was known to be approachable and a good listener. He was fair and unbiased in his deal-ings with people. The company was making substantial profits and he had initiated an employee share scheme that had pleased and motivated workers to take pride in their job and quality of work.

Paul was married to a journalist and they had one child, Thomas, who was 13 years of age. Thomas was assessed by the school psychologist as being in the top 20 per cent of the population in ability (as measured by intelligence tests). He was articulate, slightly aggressive in his manner and very stubborn. If Thomas thought an idea had no merit, he would not participate or conform. Thomas's father had recently been called to the school because Thomas had refused to wear school uniform as a result of accessing some research studies on the Internet which had shown that making young people conform crippled their creativity. He felt he had a solid and well researched argument to support his case. The school principal disagreed and promptly suspended him for a week.

Paul had to go home to prepare for a company Board meeting and was angry and frustrated by his son's position. On returning home, he had a couple of scotches and two glasses of wine with dinner as he engaged his wife in a monologue on his son's stupidity. Thomas felt that his father was unsupportive and commenced labelling him with some unpleasant and crude epithets, which caused Paul finally to lose his cool, raise his voice and give his son an earful about lack of gratitude, immaturity, stupidity and mental retardation!

Thomas seized the moment, got up from the table and told his father that he could be like the Christmas poultry and 'get stuffed'. He stormed towards the front door, shouting back at his parents that he was going out. His father demanded that he stay at home but the front door slammed and Thomas disappeared into the night. Not to be ignored, Paul grabbed his car keys and took off in pursuit of Thomas, determined that his authority would not be ignored in that way.

Four streets away, Paul encountered a mobile police breathalyser unit, was pulled over, breathalysed and found to be over the blood alcohol limit, sufficient to lose his licence for three months. Thomas had baited his father; Paul had taken the bait and paid the price.

It is my observation that very few people can successfully hold a view of themselves as both parent and adult. They behave in one way with other adults in the workplace and socially, yet inside the front door of their home, they change and behave entirely differently with their children! Their manner and

language change. The parent inside dominates their personality and the adult fades. In Paul's case, there was a high price to be paid when this occurred.

It is often said about self-esteem that the view that we have of ourselves governs how we relate to others. I suggest that the same is true of parenting. If you see yourself as a parent, you risk having your adult view of yourself go out the window. Your actions and behaviour will reflect the inner picture that you hold of what a parent should do and how they do it.

'Parents' often take on the burden of responsibility for their children. They feel the pressure. 'Adults' accept responsibility for their children without being weighed down by feelings of pressure. 'Parents' also develop amnesia regarding what they were like as children. Perhaps this is brought about by the fear that their worst characteristics have been transmitted to their children!

Once we stick the parent hat on ourselves, we also put on the burden of responsibility. Not uncommonly, we forget that we were once children and lose our sense of humour. Refusing to acknowledge our children's perspective, we often seem incapable of acting like adult human beings. We see no option but to react as parents. Yet this is a matter of choice: we *could* choose to recall the child in ourselves and feel comfortable with memories of our childhood behaviour. We could laugh at ourselves and our mischievous antics. It's our choice.

Often we are unaccepting of what we were like as children and may be too fearful to recall this publicly. We believe that to admit to our own children that our behaviour wasn't perfect is to risk seeing it repeated in the next generation. Part of the parent attitude is trying to prevent children from making the same mistakes that we made. Fear is the base of many parental words and actions.

What a combination: a life driven by fear, burdened by responsibility, loss of memory and a lack of humour. How would you like to live with someone whose life is dominated by these factors? Maybe your child does!

CASE STUDY: Like father, like son

A consequence of being in practice as a psychologist for some years is that you start to see the next generation of families. I had taught Sean some thirty years ago. I remembered him very well as an intelligent, witty and lively Year 10 student. He barely did a scrap of work but had all the charm and personality of someone who was either going to make a fortune or be on the wrong side of the law. He did in fact go on to make a fortune, having achieved a record at his university for the longest time taken by an undergraduate student to complete a degree! Formal learning never seemed to fully engage him.

There in front of me, sat Sean with his twelve-year-old son James. Sean expressed concerns about James's attitude to school, his lack of homework, his premature interest in girls. I laughed uproariously and engaged James in stories about his father. How quickly Dad had forgotten his youth! A case of 'like father, like son'! Except that father had, with the passage of time, lost his sense of humour about his childhood.

After recovering from the embarrassment of the revelations about his past, Sean realised that his anxiety was driving James into a worse situation. As I write, James has left school without completing his secondary studies and obtained an apprenticeship in the building industry, still lives at home and has a great relationship with both his parents. He is responsible and negotiates with his parents to have a social life that meets their combined needs. He is cautious about alcohol and uses no illicit drugs. James is fit and healthy.

The turning point? Sean took off his parent hat, regained his adult sense of humour and had faith that, with support from both parents, James would turn out alright. His own experience had taught him that people don't always march to the same drum. Thirteen years to gain an undergraduate degree isn't exactly the norm! My suspicion is that Sean didn't want to admit that James was capable of similar 'non-adult' behaviour. In our next session, Sean admitted that, upon reflection, 'I know I'm talking to myself when I talk to James.' The light had switched on!

Shifting from Parent Thinking to Adult Thinking

Making the shift from parent thinking to adult thinking requires work on ourselves. In common speech we talk about reaching 'adulthood' as if it were a fixed point in our lives like a station on a railway line. The perception can be that we cross an invisible line into adulthood and remain in a static state. But this perception is not true: we evolve, we change. We take unresolved issues from our childhood and adolescence into adult life, like the train that picks up and carries passengers from previous stations to deposit them, with us, at our destination.

Sometimes we don't see or recognise the parts of ourselves that are less adult. Every day is occupied with achieving 'here and now' activities. For most of us, there is little time to gaze into a mirror and reflect on ourselves. Years can go by. Beliefs and habits become well entrenched and we can become deaf to our own voice. We speak but we do not hear what we say.

Is this abnormal? Not at all. Yet if we are to become adult in our approach to our children, we need to check our status as adults. What type of adult are we? Have we done some work on ourselves to discard excess weight that we have carried from the past and that no longer serves a positive purpose. The adult within us recognises that our own self-comfort and peaceful acceptance of ourselves as adults will require us to dispose of a number of beliefs. Some of these might be:

- that other people are to blame for how I feel
- that I need to be perfect to be effective or loveable as a person
- that another person's view of me is more important than my own
- that when I make a simple mistake or fail, on occasion, to reach a goal, I have failed in some wider sense
- that I need to control my relationships with others in order to be happy
- that I need to be fearful of some things in life if I am to avoid getting hurt
- that if I do feel pain or get hurt, then I can't cope or recover.

It is beyond the scope of this book to examine in more depth the beliefs that we hold of ourselves as adults. My invitation is for you to take some time to focus on yourself and what you believe to be true about you as an adult now. How do you see yourself and life? This is a prelude to putting on your adult hat. Undertake some personal development reading, or a course.

Adulthood is not a static phase of life. Things change. We change as we grow older. Reassessing and redefining who we are is a key to our mental health. It is also a platform for building our relationship with our children. Being prepared to understand ourselves as adults will allow us to take the parent hat off.

Accept the fact that you are a biological, adoptive or step-parent – then forget the word 'parent' completely. If your sperm or egg has created the child, think of being a parent as a biological moment in your life: a brief moment of past passion that has changed your life. After the excitement and thrill (or pain) of the birth, stop seeing yourself as a parent. Accept that there is a genetic connection – a physical bond – that permanently exists between you as an adult and the child.

> *Susan looked at her nine-year-old daughter, Marianne. She was cheeky and full of life, and spent most of her waking hours listening to music and choreographing dance routines. 'Just like me', she mused; she felt comfortable with her daughter's behaviour.*

If you are an adoptive or step-parent accept that children, biologically created by someone else, are now a feature of your life. You, however, remain an adult. By doing so, you will be a more positive and potent force in the children's lives.

Chapter 3
Different Types of Parent

As of September 2008, Australia had a population of 21.4 million people who live in a variety of circumstances. Some people live on their own. Some share accommodation with others. In June 2001, the Australian Bureau of Statistics estimated that there were 7.4 million households in Australia. The number of one-person households had grown (due largely to the ageing population) as had the number of one-parent families. In 1976, 60 per cent of families were made up of couples with children; by 2001, this had fallen to 47 per cent.

The nature of families in Australia, as in many other Western countries, has changed. Consequently, there is now a wider variation among parents themselves and a correspondingly broader range of issues for parenting. Let's look at some of these.

Adoptive Parents

Adoptive parents, in my observation, are particularly susceptible to the burden of responsibility. If you are an adoptive parent, you need to acknowledge that there is a biological bond between your child and someone else. You will never share that bond. It will always exist, and will influence the sort of person that the child will become. That's reality.

As an adult, you can provide a positive environment of love and support in which the child can grow. Despite your efforts, you may see behaviours that seem (and most likely are) quite out of character with you and your partner. They probably have their roots in the connection with the biological parents. As an adult, you need to accept the reality that there will be limitations to your influence on the child – you can't fight the genes! – but you can do your best. Never let go of your love for your child.

CASE STUDY: Nature or nurture?

Anne's adopted son Darryl was different from her and her husband. He looked like them, yet he never took anything seriously. Life was to be enjoyed and spontaneity drove his behaviour. Trying to get Darryl to stick to a routine had become a lost cause. This caused tension until Anne thought of the possibility that he was probably like one of his birth parents. Investigations showed that this was true. Darryl's natural father had a long school history of difficulty maintaining a routine. He had left school in Year 10 and for most of his adult life had played in a rock band, much to the horror of his parents who still criticised him for not having a regular job.

Step-parent

In 2003, 8% of children (0 to 17 years) lived with a step couple or blended family. If you are a step-parent, you've taken on a mix of the worlds of both the biological and adoptive parent. A biological connection exists between your partner and their child, and another between you and your child. For your partner's child, you will be like an adoptive parent, but with a difference: if the absent natural parent is alive (and even if they are not), you may well experience resentment from your partner's child that you exist, let alone share a house with them and have a say in their daily routine! They didn't choose to live with you. For many step-families or 'blended families', as the jargon now has it, this will be the reality.

If you had to have one key aspect of your role in mind it would be to not attempt to be a parent to a child who is not yours. Leave the parenting to the natural parent. Just be an adult. Don't confuse the roles. Putting on a 'step parent' hat can be the first step to creating problems.

CASE STUDY: You're not my real mum

When Adrian and Michelle moved into a house with their combined family, Michelle noticed that Adrian's ten-year-old daughter Samantha ignored her. As time went by, the situation changed little. Michelle had a cold personality, and displayed little warmth. Samantha was a smiling, cuddly and expressive girl.

When Samantha was asked why she ignored Michelle, she said that Michelle wasn't her mother and that she hadn't wanted to live with her father and Michelle. She resented Michelle's presence in her life and wanted to live with her own mother. This was an issue that needed to be resolved before Samantha would accept being part of her new family structure.

As an adult, Adrian needed to acknowledge, before any progress could be made, that Samantha didn't connect to Michelle, and that this was okay.

Children experience a sense of loss when their family breaks up. Empathy for Samantha's feelings and her grieving is the first step for both Adrian and Michelle. It takes time for a sense of loss and confusion to dissipate.

Telling a child in this situation to change their attitude or to give Michelle 'a go,' or selling the child on Michelle's nice qualities will do little to ease the pain.

Single Parent

Nineteen percent of Australian children under 17 years of age live in a single-parent family, the majority living with their mother. If you are a single parent, there will be a biological connection but you will carry the weight of total responsibility for the day-to-day upbringing and welfare of the child. Your road is likely to be lonely and tiring. It is likely that you will feel mixed emotions when one of your children turns out to be 'just like his father or mother'. You need to avoid transferring onto your child the feelings you have about the partner you are no longer with.

CASE STUDY: History repeating

Erica had been attracted to Steven since they met at a school dance. After Erica fell pregnant to him the year after they left school, she and Steven married and stayed together for ten years.

Steven resented being trapped with the responsibilities of marriage and a child. He became very jealous when he saw his friends buying new cars, travelling overseas and enjoying a range of sex partners. He felt he was missing out on the joys of life.

His occasional marijuana use became regular, and his parents criticised him and blamed Erica for having deliberately trapped him with a child. Steven's frustration turned to anger and he would punch the walls or smash an item of furniture to release his feelings. Finally, Erica could take no more. She left Steven, taking her nine-year-old son with her. Supported by a single parent's pension, she took up residence in a shabby one-bedroom flat. She hated Steven for what she felt he had done to her life and her son. Money was scarce and their quality of life low.

One day Erica received a phone call from the principal of her son's school, who told her that her son had smashed school property because he became angry with his teacher. Erica felt very fearful and desperately alone. Maybe her son was a reincarnation of his father.

Gay and Lesbian Parents

Another type of parent who is little acknowledged by our society is the gay parent. The census in 1996 found that there were nearly 20,000 homosexual defacto couples living in Australia. (Prior to 1994, the Australian Bureau of Statistics did not classify a homosexual couple as a couple in its collections.) Often, because of discrimination, gay people who have children present as single parents, but they have a quite separate set of issues to deal with in their parenting role.

CASE STUDY: Keeping secrets

Frank was a 35-year-old professional, and a successful and responsible adult. After turning 16, his son Kevin had chosen to live with his father. This was despite Frank having told his family and former wife some years ago that he was gay. The situation had presented a new challenge for Frank and his partner Sean, a 30-year-old teacher. Kevin was attending a leading private school paid for by Frank. By agreement, the family had always been protective of Kevin's welfare, ensuring that only Frank dealt with school issues. However, Frank avoided close contact with teachers, school administrators and the parent association, and stayed away from school social functions. He, Sean and Kevin's mother feared that his son might suffer if it became known that Frank was gay. This caused further difficulties when Kevin's friends visited or Frank and Sean went to watch Kevin play sport. For all public purposes, Frank presented as a divorced father.

As our society matures, we may become less judgmental of gay or lesbian parents. In past decades, separation and divorce carried a stigma, but this has now disappeared almost completely. In another two decades, the stigma applied to gay and lesbian parents will also disappear, enabling them to function more effectively as adults with children.

Grandparent Families

In 2003, there were 22,500 grandparent families in Australia with children aged between 0 and 17 years. These families represented around one percent of all families with children. By comparison, in 1997, 5.5% of American children lived in a household maintained by a grandparent. While a minority-form of family, grandparent families are none the less important. These parents are usually older than in the average family and have prior experience at child-raising.

Transitional Parents

A study of Australian marriages in 1999 found that 32 per cent of all marriages were likely to end in divorce. The United States divorce rate is even higher. Marriage is a gamble – no wonder it still appeals to Australians, who have a strong disposition to 'take a punt'. Remarriages following divorce are likely to have the highest risk of divorce.

Parents who are going through a divorce often believe that it is in the best interest of the children to protect them from the stress of a breakup. And stress it is: divorce and separation are among the top three causes of stress-related illnesses, only ranking behind death of a spouse. The reality is that children living with parents who are breaking up will experience stress and pain. They don't need lies. They don't need protection from reality. They need truth, support, understanding and reassurance.

In 2003, 22% of all Australian children aged between 0 and 17 years had a parent living elsewhere. In the US, the 2000 Census discovered that 26.2% of American children and youths under 21 were in the same position.

Children are powerless when their parents break up. It is the adults who call the tune. They initiate the changes. Children tag along and are often expected to simply accept the changes and cope with them. This can be very difficult, particularly when they are living with adults who are so immersed in their own emotional turmoil that they have little to offer their children.

Individual adult reactions to separation and divorce vary. Children's reactions also vary, depending on a number of factors, including:

- the age of the children
- the intensity of the conflict between parents
- the level of emotional tension in the house prior to separation
- the degree of approval and love from both parents
- the opportunity to discuss the separation and divorce with both parents
- economic hardship arising from the separation which creates loss of opportunities
- geographical moves
- changes of school and friendship group
- the appearance of a new adult male or female in the custodial parent's life.

Simple things can cause stress for children experiencing change. Think, from a child's perspective, of the things that can change during a separation or divorce:

- routine
- school
- friendships
- bedroom
- family pets
- mealtimes
- household routines
- contact with the other parent and relatives.

A separation or divorce really requires adjustment by the children to a large number of changes. Little in their lives remains constant. It can be completely destabilising for a child who is in the process of trying to create a sense of who they are.

CASE STUDY: I can help my parents

Sophie was twelve years old when her parents Jack and Michelle decided to separate. For months there had been a cold and angry atmosphere in the home. Michelle blamed Jack for the breakdown in the relationship, and Sophie would often find her mother crying when she came home from school. Neither Jack nor Michelle had sat down to explain to Sophie what was happening – she was left guessing. One night she heard Jack yell at her mother 'Don't think I'm supporting you and the kid, you bitch.' Sophie pulled the doona over her head and cried. She felt scared. What was going to happen? 'Perhaps,' she thought, 'if I was better behaved Mummy and Daddy might be okay.'

The concept of 'family' is changing. It was only a few decades ago that a family would have been defined as two parents of opposite sex with children. This concept of the family evolved, with the increase in the divorce rate, to include a single parent with children. As single parents cohabited with their shared children, the concept of a 'blended' family was born. Now the definition has widened to embrace a homosexual or lesbian parent, perhaps with their same-sex partner, and children. Over the next couple of decades, we will see increasing debate and possibly legislative change to enable a lesbian to conceive children or homosexuals to adopt children. This will bring about the need to understand the effects on children of being raised in less traditional family structures.

Whichever type of parent we are, we can strengthen our effectiveness by assessing our situation as adults.

Parenting and Work

In addition to the type of family structure, membership of the labour force impacts upon the role of parents. In 2003-2004, according to the Australian Bureau of Statistics:

- 83 per cent of fathers living with a partner and dependent children were employed full-time
- 22 per cent of mothers living with a partner and dependent children were employed full-time

- 36 per cent of mothers living with a partner and dependent children were employed part-time.

For single parents with dependent children:

- 53 per cent of male single parents were employed full-time
- 19 per cent of female single parents were employed full-time.

For all of these groups, there is the task of juggling parenting responsibilities with the demands of employment. This can pose a special challenge, as humans do not live their lives in discrete boxes. Issues flow from home to work and vice versa. Work performance can be strongly affected by the demands of parenting. The more harmony members of the labour force can have in their home environments, the less stressed and fatigued they will be when they present at work, and the more effective and productive they will become in the workforce.

Developing more effectiveness as parents contributes to our effectiveness as workers. Stress causes a narrowing of attention, preoccupation and fatigue, each of which are contributors to workplace accidents and errors. Stress dulls the thinking process. Costly mistakes can occur. Stress contributes to poor co-worker relationships. Having stressed-out and depleted employees interacting with the public virtually guarantees alienated customers and clients. Investing in better parenting is of value to both the individual and the employer.

CASE STUDY: Who wants Andrew?

Julie was 36 years of age and employed full-time as a call centre operator for a telecommunications provider. Since her divorce from Peter, she had had sole custody of their two children, eight-year-old Andrew and eleven-year-old Rebecca.

Andrew was a restless and physically active child who seemed to be always in trouble at school. Frequently, Julie was called up to the school to discuss Andrew's behaviour. This resulted in time off work and led to conflict with her supervisor. Julie's health started to slide. Headaches became more frequent and she felt that she wanted to 'explode'. Never having been prone to depression, Julie was fearful that when she went to bed, her mind would turn to questioning the value of life.

Anyway, who in their right mind would want to take on Andrew? Her fear increased. She knew her work performance was down, she didn't trust her supervisor, and what would happen to them all if she lost her job? Life was hell.

Julie's situation is not uncommon to members of the Australian workforce. Almost one fifth of female single parents are employed full-time and many more work part-time.

The potential for stress in an attempt to juggle the roles of worker and parent without other adult support is enormous. The parent's own emotional needs are often poorly met and this impacts on their competence as a parent. Day by day their adult self retreats into a blurry memory.

A vicious circle

Home and work are not discrete, self-contained areas of life. The exhaustion of parenting impacts upon work performance. Likewise, job problems can affect a parent's relationship with their children. Research indicates that job pressures can interfere with communication between parent and child. Stressed parents tend to be preoccupied and less inclined to engage their children in conversations focused on the children's lifestyle and interests.

A challenge to employers

As society continues to change, it will become necessary for employers and workers to find ways to promote employee health by accommodating the demands of parenting. The days of Father at work and Mother at home have disappeared permanently from the social landscape. The burden of responsibility for child rearing falls on all parents, irrespective of whether or not they are in the workforce. Employers need to be sensitive in recognising this dual role of parent and worker. To do so is not only humane but recognises the increased productivity of workers who are not preoccupied with anxieties from their parenting role.

If you are an employer:

- recognise the dual responsibilities of your employee–parent
- promote a family-friendly workplace
- be prepared to negotiate with employee–parents when these responsibilities conflict.

For many workers, computer technology offers options for work to be done at home.

CASE STUDY: Family-friendly employer

Andrew and Cathy have two school-age children. Both are full-time workers and Cathy's grandparents provide before-school care in order that Cathy and Andrew can commence work at the required time.

The grandparents have gone on holidays for a week. Cathy is able to negotiate with her employer to take the children to school and commence work an hour later than normal.

In this case, her employer has the option of asking her to work later, or acknowledging that she regularly takes work home and completes it in her own time (beyond the call of duty); a third option would be to e-mail work to her at home so that she could complete necessary work within the changed hours. This would meet the needs of all parties.

Parenting and Power

Being a parent gives you enormous power: power over children who are younger and dependent on you to have their multitude of needs met. This is normal, yet by taking on the notion of being a parent, the adult can be lulled, subconsciously, into a range of parenting behaviours that can cause rather than solve problems. You can become focused too strongly on issues of control and discipline. Parents like to control and discipline their children. Control means that an external person (the parent) takes responsibility for what children do. It keeps the children within boundaries that are set and maintained by parents.

CASE STUDY: Carrying the load

Marika and Hans took their responsibilities as parents very seriously. They were both brought up in strict Catholic families and had strong respect for tradition and authority. They set the boundaries for a range of behaviours and strictly enforced them with punishment and lectures on morality. The family was united and happy until the teenage years arrived and their two children, Jan, a 13-year-old boy, and Saskia, a 15-year-old girl, became tired of their parent's rigidity.

Jan complained that he was never listened to. Saskia was tearful when recounting the pressure she felt to be perfect. Sex was never discussed. Marika was fearful of the increasing sexuality of the children. Hans was concerned that peer-group pressure would challenge parental authority in the teenage years. The burden of responsibility was weighing heavily on both Marika and Hans.

Discipline is predicated on a traditional view that the child is naturally naughty or so immature and inexperienced that they must be forced to conform. Discipline, for a parent, is something they impose on children in response to what the child has done.

Notice the past tense in that last sentence. The children do something, the parent steps in and assesses what has been done. They are reacting. If the behaviour is not appropriate, the parent then implements discipline, through a punishment. Fear often underlies the use of discipline. We hope that the unpleasant nature of the discipline that we meet out is strong enough to deter the children from doing wrong again in the future.

Now consider the following idea:

Telling your child what to do is easier than teaching them what to do.

It is also an attempt to satisfy the need for the parent to be in control. The outcome of this disciplinary and punitive approach can be quite negative. Children who are angry and resentful of parental control can act out their frustration. A simple example is the parental habit of demanding that the child do something 'because I say so'.

Telling your child what to do may seem easier than teaching your child what to do. However, the outcomes are most likely to be very different.

CASE STUDY: While the cat's away

Derek considered himself to be a conscientious and good father. His son Patrick had been a good boy until he turned 14. Derek was a traditionalist. From early in Patrick's life, Derek had insisted on strict obedience: 'I used to say to Patrick "do it and do it now", and if he answered back, I'd quickly tell him to get on with it because I'd told him to. You can't take lip from young kids.'

Patrick had evidently conformed until puberty struck but then, as he mixed more widely, he saw that his mates weren't quite as compliant with their parents as he was. He was a pleasant young man who liked to make people happy and keep the peace. He rarely argued or fought with anyone and generally respected the rights of others to have their own opinions.

Derek recounted the incident that had led him to seek help. Patrick's mate Anthony's parents were away for the weekend skiing, and had left Anthony at home in the care of his older sister. Unknown to them, Anthony's fascination with cars had led him to have a spare set of keys cut to his mother's Saab. The moment had arrived.

Anthony called up Patrick and the two of them took the Saab for a spin along the highway. Doing 100 kmh (62 mph) in a 60 kmh (37 mph) zone didn't seem all that fast to the boys, but the police differed in their view.

The expression 'because I say so' is another way of saying 'because I have the power or authority to demand that it be done'. It is a very good way of training children to act on external authority, rather than helping them develop their own set of logical rules. Beware! If you are using such expressions, you are training your child to make inappropriate decisions.

Furthermore, it is the start of creating a willingness to conform to peer-group pressure. Patrick had not thought through the consequences of what might happen if he joined his friend. When asked to recount why he became involved, he was at a loss to explain it. He had unthinkingly just gone along with his friend's request.

Parents impose discipline and control. Adults set boundaries and teach children. We'll look at this again in in Chapter 4, in the section entitled Setting Boundaries. For now, let's explore the idea of change.

To Change the Child, Change Yourself

The word 'parent' is problematic. It is laden with all sorts of messages about power, control, discipline, and an automatic right to respect and obedience. I am convinced that we would have less parent fatigue if we considered the word 'parent' obsolete. Feeling like a parent, thinking like a parent and behaving like a parent may not help your child to grow into the sort of person that you would like them to become. It also creates a tiring existence for you as the adult. A better quality of life can be regained by changing the way we communicate with our children – that is, by changing ourselves.

Can you really make such a change? Yes, you *can* choose to change yourself. The irony is that the more we direct our energy to changing ourselves, the more likelihood there is that we will see a change in our children's behaviour.

> *I can change. I can live out of my imagination instead of my memory. I can tie myself to my limitless potential instead of my limiting past. I can be my own first creator.*

—Stephen R. Covey, *Daily Reflections for Highly Effective People*

Focusing on yourself and not your child will empower you to provide an environment in which children can grow into responsible, happy and well-adjusted young adults. Interestingly, parents can exert the most influence on career plans and educational goals in teenagers. This is contrary to the general view that parents have less influence on young people's lives than their peer group.

**The only person you have the complete power
to change is yourself.**

Most parents spend much of their time thinking about and planning to change their children. Their focus and energy is directed outwards towards the children. Parents see themselves as sculptors, shaping and moulding the child into something that they see as desirable. Parents believe that it is their right, their role and their responsibility to do this. How sad!

For some parents it becomes an obsession: 'How can I make my child change his or her behaviour?' Or the plaintive cry goes up: 'If only my child would change, we would be happier'. They create a situation where the parent is powerful and the child is expected to be compliant.

Some parents don't take ownership of their feelings. It is not a mature approach to life to blame others for how you feel. If you tend to blame your children for your quality of life or lack thereof, return to the section on Shifting from Parent Thinking to Adult Thinking on page 25 and reflect on your belief system as an adult. There is no harm in having the desire to modify your child's behaviour, but there is no acceptable way to *force* your child to change. Yet for many parents, hours of wasted energy are spent plotting and planning to force a child to cooperate or modify their behaviour. And there is no limit to the depths that parents will sink in order to do so.

CASE STUDY: Super-sleuth parents

James and Eileen seemed to be reasonable people. James was a successful plumber with 12 employees. Eileen did the books in the business and they appeared to be making a dollar. The marriage was stable and there was no apparent trauma in the family.

Simon, their middle child, was different, in their view, to the other two. Eric, the eldest child, was at university pursuing a degree in engineering. Susy was in Grade 6 and was described in school reports as a 'sheer delight', a view endorsed

by her parents. Simon, on the other hand, was a different kettle of fish. At 14 years of age and a height of 184 cm, he was full back in the local football team and didn't think schoolwork had much to offer. He reminded James of his grandfather, a highly decorated soldier in the First World War. James and Eileen valued education and although they never admitted it, deep down there was a bit of inter-family competition with Eileen's brother, whose children attended the same schools and were all doing 'very well'.

Dissatisfied with his academic performance, the parents conspired to motivate young Simon. They monitored every second of his time, listened in to his telephone calls and went through his bedroom and checked for drugs when Simon was at school. They called up Simon's classmates' parents to check on what their children said Simon did at school, and interrogated Simon's brother and sister about his life. Simon felt that he was being stifled and betrayed. One night he went out and, in an attempt to relieve his frustration and sense of powerlessness, got drunk and was hit by a car while staggering home. The next five weeks were spent in hospital. What did he learn? He learned to hate his parents even more because of the pain and suffering he was experiencing. His parents took the view that the fact that he had been hit by a car validated their suspicion of him and their own behaviour towards him.

Even over time, James and Eileen could not change their view of what they were doing. They were the parents, and their desire to cling to that label was more important than building a relationship with their son. Simon dropped out of school, avoided his parents by staying away from home at every opportunity and had little sense of future direction.

The reality of life is that you can only change yourself. In the process of giving attention to the one area over which you have total power – your own behaviour, attitudes and values – you will usually see a response from others around you. In other words:

As I change the way I act or react to others, I will see others changing.

Focus on how you respond when faced with different behaviours from your child. What buttons does your child push in you? They are testing you: challenging your status as an adult or parent. You can choose to use these challenges to your status as an adult or parent to teach children about responsibility and decision-making, or you can choose to have your confidence in yourself eroded.

As an adult, why should you choose to get upset by a child's not behaving appropriately? You don't have a problem. The child does. Why would you want to own their problem? As an adult you are in the position to use the opportunity to educate the child regarding more appropriate behaviours. Parents are into 'disciplining'. Discipline usually means punishment. Parents wait for a child to make a mistake and then step in after the event, and use their power to apply a punishment. In these circumstances, parents are usually very emotional, which in turn unleashes the child's emotions. The result? Emotional exchanges and little clear thinking or focus on the core issue.

Adults are into teaching their children. Adults use their own accumulated experience to provide learning experiences for their children. It is a two-way deal – adults teach children and children teach adults. The feedback you receive from your children helps you to grow and mature as a person. This rarely happens for people who wear the parent hat. They are too easily threatened by a child's view of themselves or their decisions.

> *The value of marriage is not that adults produce children, but that children produce adults.*

—Peter De Vries, novelist (1910–93), *The Tunnel of Love*, 1954

Life's experiences are rarely all good or all bad. They are a mix of both. Looking back on your own life with a degree of honest reflection, you will identify good decisions that you made from which you reaped a reward. Likewise, embarrassingly, there will be memories of stupid decisions and actions that caused you pain. Hopefully, the person that you are today will reflect your capacity to have learnt from both your good and bad decisions. Why? Because both types of decisions had outcomes. The good outcomes may have led to further actions on your part to improve your quality of life. The bad outcomes may have led to future choices deliberately designed to avoid future pain and suffering.

 ## CASE STUDY: Alcohol abuse

At 19 years of age, Michael was a hot-headed young man, who, in his own words, 'took no shit from no-one'. In a nightclub one night, a stranger insulted his masculinity by calling him a poofter. His temper, fuelled by alcohol, exploded and Michael hit out at the individual, causing severe wounds as the beer glass he was holding punched into the man's right arm. The outcome was permanent nerve damage to the arm and hand, and a short jail sentence for Michael.

This was not an experience that Michael ever imagined he would have. He decided to look at his situation and joined an Alcoholics Anonymous group that met within the jail. On his release, he remained in contact with Alcoholics Anonymous and decided to remain sober 'one day at a time'. He returned to study and qualified for entry to a university degree in social work. His goal is to work with violent young people who need help in developing anger management skills.

A sad story? Not necessarily. Michael learned that decisions have outcomes. It was a painful learning experience that sadly affected another person's life. A step in Michael's personal growth was to acknowledge the effect he had had on another person and to feel remorse for the pain he had caused. Michael took that experience and turned a mistake into a success.

Chapter 4
Decisions, Decisions

Strange as it may seem, decisions are rarely based on logical reasons. As humans, we try to satisfy our various needs by juggling our thinking and feelings. Sometimes, thinking wins. At other times, feelings may sway the decision. Understanding how decisions are made will help you teach your child to make good decisions.

If you live with a teenager, you will probably be familiar with the teenager who goes to the local video store to get a movie and then returns home with seven movies. When asked why they got seven movies, the answer is: 'Oh, it was cheaper to get more than one!' The fact that there is no time to watch seven movies hadn't entered into the decision-making. Oh well, it felt good at the time they were in the video store! (Perhaps you've found yourself doing the same thing!)

CASE STUDY: Tyre-kicking with Dad

Tina wanted to buy a car. She had just turned 18 and gained her driver's licence. Tina and her father spent many weekends touring car yards and looking at cars. Tina visualised herself in a red or yellow sports car. It would have to be automatic, with a sunroof and a CD player. She had $7000 to spend, having saved up her money from a part-time job that she had held through the last three years of her secondary education.

There were very few cars that met all of Tina's criteria. Those that did had done in excess of 150,000 km (93,000 miles), and her father cautioned her about repair bills and the reliability of such cars. Tina was angry. She refused to look at any more cars, and for the next six weeks didn't mention the purchase of a car.

In the seventh week, Tina suggested to her father that they look at something a bit different and she looked at a wider range of cars, finally selecting a six-year-old four-cylinder car that had been well cared for by its elderly owner. She purchased it for $5000 and, six months later, the car is going well and Tina is happy.

Notice in Tina's situation the stages that she went through in making her final decision:

- She started with a dream. She visualised the type of car that would make her feel good.
- She had knowledge of what she could afford to spend.
- She was angry that her needs wouldn't be met within her budget and withdrew from the decision-making process.
- Tina's father didn't take on the burden of responsibility but waited for Tina to resume the quest for a car. He had learnt the power of silence.

- Having given herself space to rebalance her thoughts and feelings, Tina resumed decision-making.
- She finally balanced feelings and thought to create a positive decision.

CASE STUDY: Not-so-easy rider

Max had dreamt for years of the motorbike he would own. He was 19 years old and doing very well in his plumbing apprenticeship. He could comfortably afford to spend $9000, but the bike that caught his eye had all the features he had ever imagined. It was only $14,000! He couldn't really afford it and repayments would be difficult because of other commitments.

'Who cares?', thought Max, 'It'll work out! I can't wait to ride it.' Six months later Max fell short in his repayments to the bank and the bike was repossessed. He blamed the bank. Today, he banks with another bank because of the injustice he believes the first bank did him.

In Max's case, notice the path he took in making a decision:
- He started with a dream.
- He had knowledge of what he could afford to spend.
- He allowed the feelings of excitement to overtake his thinking.
- He chose to take an unnecessary financial risk.
- He made a decision solely based on feelings.
- The outcome of Max's decision was short-lived.
- He took no responsibility for the outcome and blamed the bank.
- Max achieved little positive benefit from his decision.

Every parent I have met has wanted their child to be a responsible person. How do they become responsible? By learning to understand the reasons behind decisions and then being given the opportunity and time to *make* decisions. And that occurs when the adult with whom they live provides them with opportunities to develop those skills.

Responsible individuals have learnt to discipline their thoughts and emotions. Throughout their childhood and adolescent years, the individual has been provided with opportunities to acquire knowledge and skills that are empowering:

The undisciplined mind is like an elephant. If left to blunder around out of control, it will wreak havoc. But the harm and suffering we encounter as a result of failing to restrain the negative impulses of the mind far exceed the damage a rampaging elephant can cause. Not only are these impulses capable of bringing about

*the destruction of things, they can also be the cause of lasting
pain to others and ourselves.*

—The Dalai Lama, *Ancient Wisdom, Modern World*

A disciplined mind comes from learning the skills of inner control. Self-discipline pays dividends. Externally imposed discipline, which usually has a punitive basis, is a poor substitute. If you commit a crime you are punished. It is far better not to commit the crime in the first place!

Children need adults who can teach them the skills necessary for making appropriate decisions. Start when children are young with simple and safe everyday situations.

Decision-making Skills

To repeat an earlier point, the word 'parent' is laden with all sorts of ideas about power, control, discipline and automatic rights to respect and obedience. An adult will earn respect. A parent *expects* respect as an automatic right. Do yourself and your children a favour and forget the word 'parent'. Stop thinking like a parent and new opportunities will emerge for you in the ways in which you can work with your children.

CASE STUDY: Involving the child

Terry was troubled by his ten-year-old son's peer group. He perceived them to be lazy, passive and low-achieving. Their attitudes, in his view, were starting to rub off on his son Damien. As an adult, Terry knew that environment had an effect on people and what they achieve.

Rather than choosing to give his son a lecture about friends and their influence, Terry and his wife Margaret chose to plan ahead and research secondary school options for their son. Margaret was actively involved in the primary school's Parents and Friends Association and was able to find out from other mothers about the schools they were selecting for their sons. Armed with this information, Terry and Margaret researched available school options and presented their son with an opportunity to visit selected schools. With each visit, they linked the school to areas of interest that their son had developed. They spoke about the music and sporting facilities and programs and suggested how much he would enjoy them.

Slowly and effectively, their son's appetite was whetted and he, in conjunction with his parents, selected a school that few of his friends were going to attend. Now, some three years later, Damien is in Year 8, happy, involved and doing well at all levels: academically, socially, in sport and in music.

Consider the steps taken by Terry and Margaret in dealing with their concerns:
- They observed their child's behaviour.
- They thought about what was happening to their son.
- They used their prior experience as adults.
- They collected information.
- They presented their son with options.
- They involved their son in reviewing the options (this is a key step).
- They built on and used their son's interests to facilitate a decision.
- They took plenty of time to solve the issue.
- They didn't communicate their fear or worry to their son.
- They encouraged their son to take part in the decision-making.

In arriving at a decision, they had taught their son valuable decision-making skills. Consider these ideas:

Children are thinking people who have little experience.
Adults have the experience.
When adults share their experience, children learn.

At times you will witness children acting emotionally but as an adult you can help them to deal with the emotion by choosing not to respond to it directly. Stay focused on the key issue. Your focus is on controlling the expression of your own emotions.

Getting a Child to Do What You Want

The young child who is brought up aware of the benefits of doing what they are being asked to do is able to develop a pattern of thinking and an awareness of the world that will be the foundation to their own style of decision-making.

Making effective decisions is a prelude to successful living. Each thing that a child does is an opportunity for them to develop skills in decision-making. From simple household tasks or chores, to homework and friendships, opportunities abound. Let me give you an example. Take the simple issue of cleaning up a roomful of toys scattered around the floor.

You might say 'Clean up your room *now*.' Your child will immediately think 'Why?' This is a very natural and intelligent response. Your child may be involved in a game that is very important and enjoyable to them. They have little knowledge or awareness of the household timetable and do not see the degree of urgency expressed by the parent. Naturally, they will express their curiosity and seek further information by asking 'Why?'

The intelligent parent *rejoices* in the child's question. It is evidence of a capacity to think and take responsibility for interacting with the world. The impatient parent responds with 'Because I've told you to and your room's a mess'.

How satisfactory is the above response for a child? Most unsatisfactory. All they have learnt is that the reason you do something is because someone tells you to do it.

But hold on, I hear you say, the parent did give a reason: 'the room is a mess'. True, the parent stated the observation that the room was untidy, but how does that connect, in the child's mind, to cleaning it up *immediately*? It could be cleaned later and everyone would be happy. Children are thinking people; they seek to make sense of what they are being asked. In this case, the response is unhelpful to their quest for meaning or learning. Now consider this communication:

' Please clean up your room, in the next twenty minutes, so that we can go out. Then, when you come home, your toys will be easy to find and we won't have an accident tripping over them. We wouldn't want to hurt ourselves and damage a toy would we? Owning toys is a responsibility.'

The parent is making the request and attaching clear benefits to the request: not having to clean up when they get home, preventing an accident and not breaking a favourite toy. Notice that the parent has clearly stated that it is a responsibility owning toys. Responsibilities continue into adult life. Today a toy, tomorrow a car!

The Fine Art Of Negotiating

Consider this technique:

- Make a request.
- Set a time limit.
- Give a reason for doing it.
- Illustrate the consequence.
- Reinforce the lesson: responsibility.

Your child may want to negotiate to finish a game before cleaning up.

That's fine. Negotiation is a skill that successful adults need and use. This is good training. Parents who are into power will be fearful of entering a negotiation because they might lose. Why? Because such parents feel the need to maintain their power base. They usually convince themselves that this is okay, because the child needs it!

In the example, notice that a time frame has been built in to the request. By planning ahead, the parent has allowed twenty minutes for the child to perhaps finish the game and also clean up. There is also time to talk it through a bit more if the need arises. Less rush, less panic and more is achieved in training the child for future life. Positive seeds have been sown.

Don't be afraid to take the time to negotiate with your child on important issues. And remember – negotiation is a process:

- Sit down together.
- Take turns in talking.
- Listen to each other without interrupting or making comments.
- When everyone has expressed their view, summarise the opinions.
- State the goal of the negotiation: that everyone should have their needs met as much as possible.
- Discuss.
- Fine-tune until a compromise that is agreeable to all is reached.
- State the agreement again clearly, so that no-one is in doubt about what is happening.

When Negotiation Fails

Children may be totally uncooperative and absolutely refuse to undertake the task. What can the parent do? Many parents would raise their voices and demand that children act immediately. They become emotional, as Derek would have done in the case study 'While the cat's away'. A short-term goal might be achieved but what is the long-term price?

Raising your voice is an effective way of creating conflict and ill feeling. Shouting voices create a tense atmosphere. The parent will rapidly engage children in a power conflict. There will be mutually bruised feelings and resentment will emerge. As parents, we can become so focused on winning at all costs that the real issue becomes lost in the conflict. We are hurt by the obstinacy of children, and children can end up hating the parent for the way in which they have been treated.

A more successful way of dealing with the situation would be to use the rtunity positively to teach children about decision-making and choices. Every choice we make in life has an outcome. Think about your life and some of the major decisions you have made, and ask yourself what the outcomes of those decisions have been.

When did you decide to change jobs? What was the outcome? Did you achieve more or less satisfaction? When did you decide to get married? What changes has that decision brought to your life? Both big choices and little choices have outcomes.

Decisions and Their Outcomes

The earlier children learn and understand the relationship between decisions and outcomes, the better equipped they will be in learning to take control of their life. They will avoid a victim mentality that results from a lack of understanding that we have choices. They will understand that the way they make decisions from the available choices will have an impact on their lives.

Understand that part of learning this connection will be that children will make mistakes. These mistakes are essential to long-term learning.

All children will try and avoid responsibility for their choices. It is much easier to blame something or someone else for what they have decided no to do. This usually occurs with high levels of emotion. Children will often scream such things as 'it's not fair,' 'I'm sorry,' 'I did it yesterday,' 'my sister is a bitch.' Children hope that the parent's attention will be deflected from the fact that something hasn't been done.

It is a smart parent who understands that avoidance behaviour is frequently an attempt to remain a child and represents the child's reluctance to take responsibility. It's all part of growing up.

Two things are important for you as the parent, in these circumstances:

1. Keep emotional control of yourself. Don't let the child's emotional outburst trigger you into saying something that is not constructive.

2. Use a script like: 'Sweetheart, what did you choose to do? Why blame me? You *chose* not to do what you had to do.'

CASE STUDY: School friends

Mary is in Grade 4. Her best friend Amanda has turned against her and decided to mix with a new group of friends. Mary is excluded by Amanda and her new friends from playing with them at lunchtime. Mary is very hurt and feels angry towards Amanda. 'What can I do?' she thinks to herself. Various options run through her mind. She could poison Amanda's sandwiches, hit Amanda, trip her up, punch her, spread rumours about her mother to the class or ignore her and start making new friends in the group.

Each of the options available to Mary has an outcome. Poisoning Amanda might lead to her death and Mary doesn't like that idea. It seems a bit severe. Tripping her up or punching her might lead to Mary getting hurt as Amanda is a very big girl and much stronger than Mary. Spreading rumours sounds like fun because that will really get to Amanda. However, as she thinks upon this possibility, she is reminded of what her grandmother used to tell her about speaking ill of people. Maybe not, thinks Mary. Ignoring her and choosing to get on with life sounds like the way to go. Mary chooses to do so and the outcome is that Mary makes new friends and discovers that she is more popular than she thought.

Mary has had a big lesson in choices and the impact that choices can have on her life. Throughout her life, Mary will continue to make choices. Even adult children sometimes need to be reminded of choices.

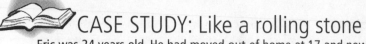

CASE STUDY: Like a rolling stone

Eric was 24 years old. He had moved out of home at 17 and now he decided to move back in with his mother. His father had discovered the fifth love of his life and decided to move out and live with her. Eric had completed Year 12 and dropped out of university to pursue his dream of being a rock star. He was playing in a well respected band that was working four nights a week and providing him with a respectable income. Yet his mother perceived an unstable aspect to her son's involvement in the music industry.

Their counsellor clearly recalled a session with them after a domestic crisis centred around the different lifestyles of mother and son. Mother, having worked herself up to an emotive state, looked at her son and exploded: 'Go out and do what you want to do now. Don't come home when you are forty with receding hairline, hair pulled back in a pigtail with stubby shorts, rubber thongs, a stud in the ear and a beer gut and say: 'Hello Mum, here's my two kids. The marriage has broken up' – I'm telling you in advance, the answer is "No!".'

Ignore the fears that Eric's mother has that create the stereotypical picture of a member of the rock and roll industry. In her own language, she is saying: 'If you choose to engage in this lifestyle and get yourself into trouble, be aware that I will not take responsibility for the consequences.' Perhaps, deep down, she is remembering her own experience in marriage. Eric's mother has made the transition from parent to adult!

Peer-group Pressure

Peer-group pressure is pressure to conform applied by a person of the same age as your child. In early adolescence, both males and females worry about being different from their friends. Conformity is the norm. A positive effect of the peer group occurs where the group are keen to learn, to do well at school and to get involved in extra-curricular activities. Conforming in such a group can have benefits for your child.

If your child has not been taught to have confidence in their ability to understand choices, they can be vulnerable to the negative effects of peer-group pressure. They have not been taught to make decisions and to see the outcomes or consequences of those decisions. They have probably always been obedient to the command of an external person – parent or teacher – and have not had sufficient experience of working through issues and taking responsibility for their decisions. They naturally transfer their compliance onto a group. The group must be obeyed.

I do not believe that the common parental cry 'My child got involved with the wrong group and the group led my child astray' has a scrap of validity. The adult recognises that it is the child's lack of confidence in making decisions that is the causal factor, not the group. Children choose to pursue activities with a group. Children's needs are met by participation in the group.

For some children who have been alienated by peers and finally find peer-group acceptance, there is a risk that conformity to the group will occur.

CASE STUDY: I wanna be like you

Rochelle was a pleasant girl. She was very attractive, cooperative in class and gained good grades in her schoolwork. Her class was dominated and controlled by a very powerful girl, Alice, who determined who was included in the social group. Alice didn't like Rochelle. Simply, the boys found Rochelle to be more attractive. Rochelle was excluded from the group at lunchtimes and felt very lonely. Another class member invited Rochelle to her home and slowly Alice was persuaded to include Rochelle in a social event that was being planned. Alice thought that it was better to have Rochelle on side so that she could have more control. The evening of the party arrived and Rochelle was to be included. Even though the group was only fifteen years old, alcohol was freely available. Rochelle felt included for the first time, but was very nervous. During the evening Rochelle drank the vodka and orange juice that was offered very quickly. By the time her father picked her up she was quite drunk.

Rochelle was not a disobedient or rebellious person. Her intoxicated state was directly related to her need to be included by her peer group. She simply did not want to be different.

Her parents were appalled by the state of their daughter. Her mother was very judgmental and blamed the group. Her father was more understanding, and appreciated the difficult circumstances that Rochelle was experiencing.

The next day he gently talked to her about the experience and Rochelle acknowledged that she had paid the price for too eagerly wanting to be accepted by her peers. It was a learning experience for her and over the next few weeks she developed her own appreciation of her position. Rochelle decided that acceptance by the girls in her class was less important than feeling good and staying in control of herself. Relationships with the girls in her class remain fairly poor.

Since this occasion, Rochelle has been to numerous parties. Mostly, her social life has been the result of invitations by various boys and her membership of a group outside of school, the local lifesaving club. She remains very cautious about alcohol and is very much in control of what she drinks. Normally, when attending a party, Rochelle will pour her own drink or open a can of soft drink herself to avoid the potential of someone spiking her drink. Her increasing self-confidence and acceptance of herself as a person has developed as a result of understanding her position within the group of girls at school and her willingness to establish her own identity outside of the school group.

The best prevention for the negative effects of peer pressure is to teach children how to make a decision from a very young age. It is too late to leave teaching of decision-making until the child reaches puberty. Let them rehearse the skills as often as possible and at a young age. By so doing, they develop confidence in their decision-making. They act and appear more confident to their peers, and are less subject to intimidation and harassment from their peers. They will develop an inner courage to trust their own decision-making skills.

Developing Decision-making Skills

If children make a wrong decision, use the experience to teach them. Allow children to learn from their mistakes. It is a learning experience, not a disciplinary experience. Here are a few words that I often find useful:

> *To see someone fall (which will teach him not to fall again) when a word from you would keep him on his feet but ignorant of an important danger, is one of the tasks of the teacher that calls for special energy, because holding in is more demanding than crying out.*

—Spoken by Simon Darcout in *Rebel Angels*, by Robertson Davies

CASE STUDY: Sex and the single boy

Freddy has just turned 15. During the last 12 months he has discovered that he is attractive to the opposite sex. Each night, the home telephone rings frequently. Each time one of his parents answers, a panting female asks for Freddy. His parents are now becoming concerned that his interest in his father's Playboy magazines is now transferring to real females. What are they going to do? Sex and study, in their view, don't mix too well.

One Saturday night, his parents return home earlier from a party than they had expected to discover Freddy in bed with his girlfriend. Mother goes hysterical, sobs and screams and throws the young lady out of the house and promptly rings her parents.

Father reads the riot act and bans his son from any telephone calls or social contact. The outcome: Freddy runs away from home. His girlfriend, fearful that she is going to lose Freddy, takes herself off the contraceptive pill and falls pregnant to him.

Think about this situation. The outcome of acting as parents has not been to anyone's benefit. How could the situation have been handled in an adult, rather than a parental, way?

The differences between a learning experience and a disciplinary experience can be summarised as follows:

Learning experience
- Your child is involved in decision-making.
- Your child understands the consequences of possible decisions before implementing them.
- They take personal responsibility for actions and their outcomes.
- The result is unlikely to result in resentment of others.

Disciplinary experience
- Another person has the power over your child and makes the decision for them.
- The action or behaviour is followed by a punishment.
- The result potentially causes resentment.
- It focuses the child's attention on the punishment rather than the behaviour that caused it.
- It rarely helps your child to become more responsible.

If Freddy's parents had invested more time in teaching him how to make a decision at a younger age, there would have been a very different outcome.

It's Never Too Early to Start
Self esteem and personal confidence, so critical in offsetting the negative influence of a peer group, is built on earlier childhood experiences of learning to make decisions. Remember that the pathway to effective decision-making will involve the younger child making errors. As an adult, use the child's errors of judgement as a learning experience. Don't slip back into the old parental thinking that you must discipline or punish the child. Ask the child: 'What have you learnt?'

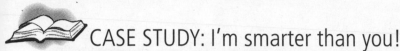 CASE STUDY: I'm smarter than you!

Tanya was a beautiful and intelligent teenager who started lying to her parents. When asked why she did so, she articulately explained that her parents 'told her what to do and what not to do because she wasn't yet 17'. She saw no logic in her parents' commands but was powerless to make a decision, so she went about doing her own thing behind her parents' backs. More and more she was being drawn to the views of her peer group because they expressed what she inwardly felt: the need to make her own decisions. Her parents noticed the change but just thought she was growing up. They believed that 'all teenagers go through that stage'. What they hadn't appreciated was that they were training a delightful young woman to become rebellious and sneaky in her behaviour. This was the only way she could meet her needs.

Remember:

Just as you have needs, so does your child.

Teach them to meet their needs in a responsible and effective way. That is your responsibility as an adult.

Setting Boundaries

Let's return to our earlier example of the young child cleaning up their bedroom. Children often hold the view that 'It's my room to do what I want with.' It will take patience for the child to develop an understanding of the adult's need for order.

If the child is totally obstinate and is not cooperating, then this is a wonderful opportunity for you to teach them more about life. It is not a disciplinary issue but a teaching opportunity. This is a key step in moving from parent to adult. Don't immediately respond as a parent. Stand back, reflect and see the opportunity for teaching. Say to the child:

'You can choose to help by cleaning up your room and make your room safer or you can choose not to. The result of not cleaning up your room will be that you will lose the privilege of playing with your toys. The choice to be responsible or not responsible is yours.'

If necessary, repeat the same statement a few times. Stick to the script that:

'If you choose to cooperate there is an outcome; if you choose not to cooperate there is an outcome as well.'

Your child is now positioned to think through the choices and the decision that has to be made. The worst possible outcome is that you have to look at a messy room whilst the child learns from the experience of choosing not to cooperate.

This is called 'boundary setting' or 'limit setting'. A limit provides a safety zone. Speed limits on a roadway are designed to provide a zone of safety in which vehicles can travel. It is not a guarantee of safety. We still have to live with a certain level of fear.

Fear is an emotion that parents, as adults, need to wrestle with and control. Setting boundaries responsibly and not exerting power is a key skill. This boundary setting is important in helping children to feel confident, safe and empowered by their choices.

Notice the subtle difference between boundary setting and exerting power by laying down the law. Laying down the law and using your sense of power is an emotional exercise in determining who has the power and who is going to win. Parents can very easily become judge and jury.

There is a reality to boundaries. The physical world has boundaries. Your dwelling and the block of land on which you live have boundaries: walls and fences. Suburbs and cities have boundaries. Countries have boundaries. Life has boundaries. Bungy jumping off a bridge might be pushing the boundaries. Jumping off a bridge without a suitable attachment is unquestionably pushing the boundaries to the point of self-destruction. Experimenting with a marijuana joint might be pushing legal and social boundaries. The latest research on marijuana also suggests that if there is a dormant genetic disposition to mental illness, marijuana use may trigger a mental condition. Choosing to use marijuana may be pushing the boundaries of good health. Your child needs to be aware of the potential and unknown consequences of their decisions. Injecting heroin is a sure way to test life to the limit.

Social relationships like family membership also have boundaries. When, as an adult, you set a boundary or limit for your young child, you can do so by logically referring to a range of factors. Explain unemotionally and clearly the purpose and nature of the boundary. Articulate to the child how everyone in the family benefits from the boundary. Illustrate how boundaries within the family are mirrored in the outside world of school and society.

Boundaries provide a sense of security. As your child grows and matures, boundaries can change. They can be renegotiated.

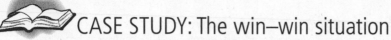

CASE STUDY: The win–win situation

Tony wanted to go to a party. He was 16 years of age. His parents weren't all that happy about it as they had strong suspicions that there would be alcohol there. They were fearful of what might occur. Their parental instincts were to lay down the law and say that he couldn't go. However, they knew from prior experience that such an action would only lead to arguments and resentment. Tony had to learn how to cope and they could teach him.

After some discussion between themselves, Tony's parents decided on reasonable boundaries. They sat down with Tony and stated their concerns and what they perceived to be reasonable responses to those concerns. Tony didn't quite agree that he should call them halfway through the evening, or that his father should come inside to pick him up at 12.30 am. How embarrassing would that be? His father looking like a slob in his old tracksuit!

Negotiations led to compromise. Tony could take a couple of light beers. It was agreed that Tony would call his parents if the need arose and his father would meet him outside the house at 1 am. Tony's father talked calmly to him about opening his own drinks and not accepting drinks poured by other people. He also explained the benefit to the family of not having to have an anxious evening worrying about whether Tony would be drunk.

Consensus had been reached in a calm fashion. Tony was picked up by his father at the agreed hour. He was sober and pleased with the night that he had enjoyed. As our corporate friends would say, it was a win–win situation.

The key ingredients in the strategy used by Tony's parents were:
- recognising their own fear, based on prior knowledge of what teenage parties can be like
- resisting the temptation to use their fear as an excuse to lay down the law to their son
- acknowledging that Tony was growing up and would need to learn to cope in a variety of situations that he encountered
- discussing the situation with each other before involving their son in discussions
- negotiating with their son and taking into account how he felt
- his father's sharing of his knowledge as an added safety factor
- clearly defined responsibility for both parents and child.

The Benefits Of Decision-Making

A person who can't make a decision is making a decision.

—René Descartes

One very positive benefit of educating our children in making choices is that they learn to take responsibility for their actions. We are deliberately encouraging responsible behaviour.

The second positive benefit of this technique is that we don't have to resort to punishments and threats. Punishment inflicted by one person is the result of them wielding power over another person. Punishment inflicted on oneself, as the result of a poor choice, is a good learning experience: there is no one to blame except yourself. Children can wail and gnash teeth and as adults, all we have to do is feed back to them that they feel as they do because of the decision they made:

'You chose not to clean up your room. Don't blame me. You were the one who made that decision. Next time, you might choose to be more cooperative and save yourself a lot of unhappiness.'

Keep in mind that this process helps children to own their feelings. A responsible adult takes ownership of their feelings and doesn't go around blaming everyone else in the world for how they feel. To achieve this as an adult we need to start developing the skill in childhood.

Learning The Script

Write the script down on a piece of paper and repeat it in a variety of situations:

'If you choose to do ..., then you also choose to ...'

An example might be 'If you choose to eat with your hands at the dinner table, you are also choosing not accompany the family when we next eat out.'

Choosing involves your child's being part of the process of setting boundaries in consultation with you. Explaining the wider social benefits of using cutlery would be an important ingredient in boundary setting.

You're The Teacher, So Teach Yourself

The more you see your role as an adult with a capacity to teach, the more positive things will occur for you and your child. Notice the difference between adult–teacher language and parent language. The words we use and how we say them are critical to our success as parents.

Exercise
Develop your skill by trying the following examples.
Parent language: 'Derek, if you are not home on time, you will not go out for the rest of the term. You'll stay at home.'
Adult language: _____

_____

Parent language: 'Michael, if you don't do your homework now, I'm going to confiscate the television set.'
Adult language: _____

_____

By virtue of their age, parents have more experience than children. Remind yourself that you are an adult who has knowledge and skills that you can teach your child. Tony's father did this when he outlined the issue of not accepting a drink poured by someone else. His prior experience had taught him how easy it is to spike an open drink. Whether you have learnt anything about being successful will be a reflection of your own maturity.

You are an adult who is your child's main teacher. Repeat it to yourself. Change your self-image:
- I am an adult.
- I am a teacher.
- My role is to teach my child to make responsible decisions and to see to the outcomes of those decisions.

If a child asks 'Why?', it is not an irritation, it is a joy. A curious child is an intelligent child and in this world you need some intelligence to survive. Nurturing and developing that intelligence is possible. The child's thinking skills will grow with experience of using them.

A question or challenge from a child is
a cue for a parent to teach.
If I teach, the child can learn.
It is through learning that the child grows.

Let's return to our exercise. Here are some suggested responses. Check them against your responses.

Parent language: 'Derek, if you are not home on time, you will not go out for the rest of term. You will stay at home.'

Adult language: 'Derek, you can choose to come back after our agreed time, in which case you will be choosing not to go out next week. Or you can get back on time and we may consider increasing your curfew next week.'

Parent language: 'Michael, if you don't do your homework now, I'm going to confiscate the television set.'

Adult language: 'Michael, if you choose to continue watching the television and choose not to start your homework, you are choosing to lose your right to watch television.'

Notice the key differences in style:

- The parent style is based on power: 'I have more power and authority than you do and I will use my power if you don't toe the line.'
- The parent style is based on threats of punishment: 'If you don't do what you are told then a punishment will be forthcoming.'
- The adult style is based on always recognising that your child has a choice. They can continue to do what they are doing or they can take responsibility for their actions and behave in a more effective way.

The adult style involves a risk on the parent's part. The child may not choose to be responsible and may continue to do what they are doing. This is not threatening if you can stand back and see that this is a learning experience for the child. Everyone, at times, will make errors of judgement, and your child is no different.

The adult style has a built in consequence for the child. Each decision the child makes will have an outcome and the outcome is clearly and logically described in advance.

The key is the content of the message. You can choose different words to express the message. Just check that the key ingredients are there:

- Use the word 'choose'.
- Offer your child a logical outcome as part of what you say (e.g. a logical outcome of playing with a knife might be cutting yourself or hurting someone else).
- Avoid using the word 'I' or making statements about your power.

Exercise

Think of a situation that you would like to change with your child. You might like to briefly record it here:

_____

_____

Now construct a statement to your child in adult language. Use a formula like this:

[First name], if you choose to _____, you are also then choosing to _____ (put in outcome).

When They Make the Wrong Choice

If children make the wrong decision, the next phase of the teaching process is to explain what has occurred. It is from learning to analyse the decisions they make and their outcomes that our children develop clearer understandings of their own behaviour.

CASE STUDY: Working out positives

Jim was very keen to get a part-time job. His school had a clearly stated policy that students were not encouraged to undertake part-time work. The school's view was that students had sufficient to do between homework and extracurricular activities.

However, Jim's parents disagreed with the school policy. They saw value in Jim learning something about work and taking responsibility for earning some cash to fund his social life and his insatiable appetite for purchasing CDs. Jim discussed his idea with his mother, Maryanne. They talked about the hours of work and agreed that 15 hours per week would be about all Jim could fit into his schedule. A vacancy became available at a fast-food store nearby. Jim applied and got the job.

'If you choose to take the job', his mother said, 'you are also choosing to keep up to date with your homework and not fall behind or get too tired.' She reminded him that she did not want to nag him about homework and being organised. Jim agreed that he could achieve that goal. He quite liked school and aspired to going to university. Neither Maryanne nor her husband Keith had had the chance to go to university and they were keen to support their eldest son in his goal.

Three months passed and Jim was very responsible in taking up the shifts that the fast-food store offered him. Maryanne was a little concerned because some of the shifts were from midnight to dawn. Jim became increasingly tired and rundown. Keith and Maryanne were anxious about his health and felt a little guilty that they were supporting their son in an activity that the school would not approve. After four months, Jim contracted a glandular-fever-type virus and was unable to go to school. Maryanne suggested that Jim should quit the job because his employer was reluctant to offer him hours that were more suitable to him getting proper rest.

It took Jim two weeks to make the decision to do that because he felt he would be a failure if he quit. After he had handed in his resignation, Keith and Maryanne sat down with Jim and walked him back through what had happened. They discussed the positive benefits of having taken the job, of having earned almost a thousand dollars, and of the experience he had gained in managing his own time and school and work commitments. Jim was disappointed but acknowledged that he couldn't keep up the pace. As a compromise, Keith and Maryanne offered to increase his weekly allowance by 20 dollars a week so that he could concentrate on his schoolwork and achieve his goal of university entrance.

In this example, the parents displayed a number of adult behaviours:
- They listened to Jim and his considered his needs.
- They discussed the options with him.
- They came to a clear agreement with Jim as to the nature of his responsibility if he made a decision to take the job.
- They gave Jim space to evaluate the outcome.
- They did not step in and use their power to demand that Jim quit his job.
- They enabled Jim to review his decision and the outcome, and to learn from them.
- They avoided any judgement of Jim.
- They recognised Jim's feelings and needs, and offered an increase in his allowance to support him in meeting his needs.

Were Maryanne and Keith wrong in supporting Jim's decision in opposition to the school policy? They held the view that the school should not dictate what a child did outside school hours. Very rarely, from some school principals' viewpoints, are adults perfect!

Selecting Sensible Consequences

When a person considers their choices and makes a decision, the implementation of that decision will lead to a result. This is called an outcome. The outcome has an effect on the person's life and may lead to other decisions being made.

With teenagers, parents are wise to enforce the consequences. Teenagers need to create the teaching moment for themselves. They learn by experience. Teenagers will not respond to lectures and questions from parents. They need to make the connections between their behaviour and the outcomes themselves. If they don't make those connections, they will simply conform in a submissive way or reject the learning and repeat the same mistakes.

Teenagers learn to be responsible for their actions by mentally working on the connection between their choices and the outcomes of those choices. This can sometimes be a painful experience and they can feel very embarrassed by it.

CASE STUDY: Alarming result

Nathan was confused. Should he go out with his girlfriend or stay at home and finish some homework? The dinner to which his girlfriend had invited him was important. Her family was celebrating her grandmother's eighty-fifth birthday. Nathan thought through his choices. He decided that he would go to the dinner and get up early the next morning to finish the important homework that was due the next day.

All went well. He came home and set his alarm clock for the next morning. But it didn't go off because the battery went flat during the night. He was late getting up, failed to complete his homework and as a result lost 20 per cent of his marks from his final score in the subject. This placed him under pressure as, the university course to which he wished to gain entry had a very high entry level. Nathan decided that as he was significantly at risk of not reaching his goal, he would have to stop his part-time job. In turn, this resulted in less income and impacted on his social life and his ability to go out.

Nathan learned a good lesson in decision-making and outcomes:
- The original decision to attend the dinner with his girlfriend and to do his homework the next morning was a valid decision.
- Nathan knew the importance of the work to be done and took a high risk in relying solely on his alarm clock.
- The flat battery cost him 20 per cent of his marks.
- To maintain his original goal, he needed to make further sacrifices.
- Nathan's social life would be radically altered for the remainder of the year because of his lack of spending money.

All because of a flat battery! Discussing his situation, Nathan commented 'Next time, I am going to be paranoid and have a back-up. In the same situation, I would book an early morning call as well as setting my alarm clock.'

Because he had learnt from his mistake, Nathan was well on the way to being a responsible young man in control of his life.

CASE STUDY: Taking a risk

Simone was 15 years old and had discovered boys. She was attractive but shy and lacked experience in understanding how boys felt and thought. Simone was a regular visitor to chat rooms on the internet and she developed a regular conversation with a 17 year-old boy in a neighbouring country. This felt safe for Simone because she could have a boyfriend without really having a boyfriend.

Over a number of weeks their internet conversation became more and more personal. They swapped photos and she thought Adrian was 'hot.' As trust grew between them, the conversation grew more intimate.

One Wednesday afternoon, Simone arrived home early as there were no classes that afternoon and connected to the internet to talk to Adrian.

Unexpectedly, Simone's mother, Michelle, came home to find her daughter naked from the waist up performing a dance movement in front of the webcam! Michelle gasped, shrieked and hastily unplugged the computer as Simone instantly disappeared clutching her bra and top in her arms.

If you were Michelle and had discovered your daughter acting in this way, how would you have responded? It would probably take a moment or two to recover from the shock!

Consider a parent response and then an adult response to this scenario.

Parent Response

Parents would be very focused on regaining control. Banning the internet, making all sorts of threats, accusing Simone of obscene and disgusting behaviour would probably be parts of the response. The situation, which is already highly embarrassing for Simone, would become emotional, if not hysterical, as emotions clashed across the room.

Adult Response

The adult would be deeply concerned, like the parent, about the nature of the behaviour and where it might lead. After focusing on controlling the very natural emotional response to what has occurred, the adult thinks about the issues before commencing a conversation with Simone. What are the issues?

1. Simone's relationship is exclusively based on internet contact. This means that there is no opportunity to check whether the other person is as they say they are. It is not uncommon for people to present themselves on the internet in a more favourable light.
2. There is a risk to Simone that, whilst she thinks she is only being seen by Adrian, there may be more than one person viewing her.
3. There is software available to capture what is transmitted by webcam. This constitutes a risk to Simone. Everything she says

or does may be recorded and later distributed through DVD or placed on the internet.

4. It may be healthier, in terms of Simone's social and sexual development, for her to be more actively involved in her own school and local community.

Simone had innocently believed that her erotic dance was only for her 'internet boyfriend.' Michelle, a single parent, quietly sat down with Simone some hours later after having consumed multiple cups of herbal tea, and she recognised her daughter felt very embarassed.

'Simone, what have you learned from this experience?' she asked. There followed a discussion about the dangers and risks of such a relationship and the type of behaviour Simone had engaged in. Michelle, with some difficulty, maintained her composure and avoided judging Simone's behaviour. Simone was shocked. Three days later, she admitted to her mother that she hadn't thought of the risks associated with what she had done.

The important outcome from this situation (and Michelle's adult focus) was the recognition by Simone that she really wanted a face-to-face real boyfriend. Two days later, Michelle and her daughter discussed how a broadening of interests and activities may give rise to exposure to a range of young males within Simone's age group.

Simone was on the first step to new social interests and new friends. She joined the local life-saving club.

Michelle trusted her daughter's intelligence that if she was given time to think and the opportunity to objectively hear what the inherent risks were in the webcam scenario, then she would be able to really assess what she wanted in her life and to make positive decisions in relation to her needs.

Imagine, for a moment, if Michelle had stuck in her parent mode. The emotional explosion between mother and daughter could have resulted in a shut-down in communication. The smouldering resentments would have taken months to extinguish.

Start Them Young

To encourage our children in the development of their ability to make decisions, we need to be mindful, from a young age, of exposing them to safe but sensible consequences.

CASE STUDY: A fair consequence

Julie was a charming seven-year-old girl. It was Moomba Festival time and her family had decided that they would go to the parade in the city. Melbourne comes alive at Moomba and there would be all sorts of entertainment along the banks of the Yarra River.

The day was planned the night before. When the family awoke, Julie was excited about the outing and decided to choose clothes to wear. Out she came from her room dressed in a colourful summer frock. Her father suggested to her that she either change her clothes or take a coat because the forecast was not promising and it might rain – a lesson any child in Melbourne, with its multiple climates each day, should be exposed to.

Julie was offended. This was the very special dress that she had been dying to wear and now her father was interfering and spoiling her plans. Stubbornly, Julie refused to change her dress or, in order to spite her father, take a coat. No fuss was made by the parents as they got into the car and drove away.

After two hours of exposure to an increasingly chilly wind, Julie started to turn a pale shade of blue and asked her father for his coat. 'I am not surprised,' replied her father. 'You chose not to listen to what I said about the weather. You chose not to bring your coat. You have chosen to be uncomfortable.' Julie became colder and started crying.

Her father, having learnt that he was not a tree and therefore wouldn't sway and bend, ignored her sorrowful tears.

When the family returned to the car Julie was extremely miserable and distressed. As her mother placed her seatbelt around her, she firmly said: 'Next time, you might choose to listen and save yourself and others a lot of pain.'

Her father did concede to put on the car heater on the way home. After all, Julie had learnt her lesson by then.

Here was a safe implementation of a sensible consequence by Julie's parents. As adults, they assessed the situation and the opportunity to teach Julie a lesson:

- Julie made a choice to wear what she wanted.
- Father provided information in relation to the choice.
- Julie chose not to take the information into account when making the decision not to take a coat.
- Father let her stay with her decision.
- Father implemented a safe consequence: not to share his coat.
- Julie experienced the unpleasant outcome of her decision.
- Mother reinforced the lesson in an unemotional manner.
- Father switched on the car heater to signify that the experience was over.

Currently, Julie is in the upper secondary level of her school, doing well academically and holding leadership positions.

Creating Reasonable Boundaries

As we saw earlier, boundaries provide frameworks in which the child can safely operate. They provide limits to behaviour. Visualise an area of land that is fenced on all sides, and on that land a horse. The horse has freedom of movement within the area but the fences define the extent of freedom that the horse enjoys. Just like that horse, a child will thrive if the boundaries are properly set.

Think about the importance of boundaries in life. Setting boundaries provides children with a space in which they can exercise freedom of choice. Importantly, the limits provide a safety net. Boundaries that are too rigidly placed may create frustration. Boundaries that are too loosely defined may be equivalent to a fence with a large gap in it through which the horse can bolt. A sense of security comes from the clear establishment of boundaries. These are the parameters within which a decision can be made. Life without boundaries can be overwhelming and very confusing.

Boundaries, in my view, should be a part of life that children grow up with from birth. Not setting boundaries during childhood and then trying to erect them when the child reaches puberty will be disastrous. The child, in these circumstances, receives a clear message that you don't trust them and that you are driven by fear. Resentment, opposition, anger and bad moods will increasingly become a part of life. Each of these can be very exhausting to live with. Your teenager will hate you and the feeling will be reciprocal!

For example, one of your values might be to accept appropriate responsibility for your child's safety. You might explain to your child that if they are visiting a friend or wish to stay overnight at a friend's house, you will want to meet the parents. Explain that the reason is one of personal responsibility on your part and a reassurance of their safety, and a courtesy to the other parents. Your child might abuse you for being over-protective and intrusive in their life. They might claim that no other parent would do this and embarrass them. Remind yourself that you are the adult. Peacefully and quietly reassert your proposition that their attendance is conditional upon you having an address and contact phone number, and if necessary meeting or talking to the other parent. Explain that for reasons of safety you have set these boundaries. Explain too that, as an adult, this is a necessary requirement on your part, which in turn results in a pleasant social opportunity for your child.

Do not waver. Do not bend. You are not a tree.

Providing boundaries for the child to consider is an important part of parenting. The child needs to take these boundaries into consideration in their decision-making. Be pleased if the child wants to discuss the boundaries and perhaps even renegotiate them. This means that the approach is working because the child is working within the framework that you have set.

If they don't wish to have a pleasant and safe time with friends, that is their choice and if they are choosing not to comply, then they are choosing to stay at home. When the child starts to get angry, ask 'What would you like to do?' This will enable the child to carry through the decision-making process.

Notice that there is a negotiating phase in this process. The child is faced with understanding boundaries, weighing up choices, developing an awareness of outcomes and taking responsibility for making a decision. Straight, calm, logical negotiating is taking place. Raised voices and excessive emotion have little place in this dialogue.

Choose not to respond or to be deflected by the unpleasant names your child may call you. Sticks and stones may break your bones but names will never hurt you. Whether you are a 'stupid old person' is not the issue. Don't play wounded parent. Keep thinking like an adult. The core issue is an acceptable agreement on how an activity is going to occur and the fulfillment of a negotiated and agreed obligation. You will agree to the activity when certain preconditions, which have their basis in logic and meeting everyone's needs, are fulfilled. These preconditions haven't been plucked out of thin air as a result of your mood. They are well thought out and logical in their construction. They take into account an understanding, by all parties, of each others' feelings and needs. Remember:

> ### Adults construct boundaries from the moment the child is born.

Logical Outcomes or Consequences Are Useful

In Julie's case, the outcome or consequences of choosing not to listen or dress appropriately were logical and carefully monitored.

In the old days a common expression was 'Let the punishment fit the crime.' Today, the more appropriate expression is 'Let the consequence fit the decision.'

In order for a child to make an appropriate decision, they need to see the logical outcomes of decisions: if you choose to leave a bath running with a plug in it, it will overflow. The consequence is a flooded bathroom. That is the natural outcome. Missing out on television as a result of flooding a bathroom would seem to be disconnected. Having to clean up the bathroom might have a more obvious connection with the original decision, and teach the child to take responsibility for the result.

CASE STUDY: Nice bloke, shame about the grades

Cameron was a student in Year 11 at a private school. He was actively involved in sport, outdoor education and school music. He was a very intelligent, personable, pleasant and well-behaved young man. However, homework held little appeal and his parents were reduced to nagging him on a daily basis about his responsibilities. Mother had a part-time job that funded the school fees. Part of her frustration was that there seemed to be little return on her investment of time and energy. Meetings were held with school staff, and the school would call up the parents with reports about what Cameron had or had not achieved. Based on these reports, Cameron would be cajoled, motivated, encouraged and further nagged by his parents. The first-semester report arrived and there were clear indications that Cameron was in difficulty academically.

If you were Cameron's parent, how would you respond? After reflection, Cameron's parents decided to abandon their 'parent' hat and negotiate with him as adults.

Cameron needed to take responsibility for his own learning. He had no learning problems, he didn't use any drugs, he liked his school and he was actively involved in his school community. There were no behavioural problems at home. It was simply a lack of work and effort that caused the poor results.

Cameron aspired to university entrance. His parents were making financial sacrifices to send him to school. They were unhappy that there was no clear benefit from their sacrifices.

It was decided that for the second semester Cameron would take full responsibility. It was agreed that he would return to the school, but that if his performance was not satisfactory at the end of the semester, he would choose to leave the school and attend a local government school to complete his studies. It was further agreed that his parents would not mention schoolwork or homework throughout the semester. Should they do so, they would pay a 'fine' of $50 to Cameron for each offence. This appealed to the parents as they had been brought up in a culture of punishment! However, Cameron was invited to ask his parents for extra support or tuition if he felt he needed it.

The result was interesting. Initially, his parents experienced difficulty in pulling back and enabling their son to take responsibility. Fear of him not succeeding led to them experiencing a couple of fines. The semester finished with Cameron achieving good grades, $150 richer and continuing on to his final year at the school.

There is a strong connection between students experiencing stress in examinations and external expectations. Students who strive for their best and place expectations on themselves experience less stress.

Teaching Decision-Making Takes Time

Choosing to be an adult who teaches your children to make decisions is also choosing to invest time in doing it. Children who are under-parented don't have parents who invest time in them. (The consequences for this group of children are articulated in Chapter 2 – see page 21). The rewards of this investment are enormous. I'll expand on this in the next chapter.

Chapter 5
The Strength to Watch Them Fail

Sometimes, as adults, we need to be courageous. Children learn by trialling different behaviours. They learn from the consequences of their actions and sometimes they need to fail. On occasions, parents may know what is best for their children. However, even though parents may know what is best, if the decision-making isn't being done by the children, learning is likely to be stunted.

As someone once wisely said:

Successful people fail, but they fail less often.

Many a successful academic, sportsperson, author and musician will testify to the truth of that statement. A school friend of mine failed Year 12. He is now a professor in a science faculty. The Beatles were told that their music was unsaleable. The 1999 European women's 400 metres champion was told, at 19 years of age, that she had no future in athletics.

How fearful are you of your child failing? Parents who are driven by fear of their children failing do crazy things like doing their homework or assignments for them. Rescuing children might make you feel good but it is bad news for them.

An adult with a secure belief in themselves is less prone to the artificial confidence boost that arises from rescuing children. The child learns nothing positive from this parental behaviour. It doesn't teach them how to become strong adults. By artificially propping up children, we teach them that the outcome of irresponsible behaviour is that someone is going to rescue them.

Children are also taught to become manipulative and to use a situation to their perceived advantage. They tend to ignore the reality of the outcome and attempt to satisfy their immediate needs. And they learn to become dependent. 'I don't have to be responsible for my homework – I can depend on Mum or Dad nagging me, harassing me or doing it for me.' This will block child's emotional growth because it is more comfortable to be dependent on a parent. They don't grow up. They stay a child.

This behaviour flows over into the child's adult relationships. Pity the partner who ends up with someone who has been well-trained by their parents to be manipulative and dependent. It is not a solid foundation for a mature relationship.

Parents rationalise their removal of the child's responsibility by saying 'I'm encouraging my child by participating in the homework.' Sadly, this is not true. Often, the child will gain the message that their parents don't believe they can do a good job themselves. This message can result in the child's self-esteem being undermined. They experience difficulty in trusting their own abilities.

I recently undertook a survey of school principals and senior staff from around Australia in preparation for a workshop for senior staff on 'social changes that impact on teachers and education.'

The findings? One of the most commonly expressed concerns was about mobile phones and how students use them. There is sufficient pressure involved in teaching young people without the added burden of monitoring mobile phone use during school hours. Yet, because of the widespread use of technology, schools have little choice but to apply policies on mobile phone use.

Children and teenagers are forgetful creatures. One of the skills that they acquire from schooling is the capacity to become organised and responsible. The common ownership of mobile phones by school students has the advantage that they can readily contact their parents (many of whom work), and *vice versa*.

The disadvantage is that there is a conveience and immediacy factor for solving acts of irresponsibility or disorganisation: a student forgets their lunch, sports clothes, homework, a textbook or a school form and the solution is easy: dial a parent and ask them to solve the problem! Most parents comply because they don't want their child getting into trouble.

The current generation of parents are rescuers.

The solution? As an adult you can accommodate the natural forgetfulness of children and also train them to become more organised and accept responsibility for what they choose to do or not do.

The technique? Three strikes and you are out.

CASE STUDY: Three strikes and you are out

Mark, at thirteen years of age, was an amiable but slightly vague child. His head always seemed absorbed with thoughts that were disconnected from the here and now. He was oblivious to time, oblivious to mess, and always seemed surprised when his mother asked him 'Are you ready for school tomorrow?'

Her question would always elicit a vague response; 'Yeah ... of course.' The reality was that every week Mark would SMS his mother in a panic over some forgotten item and plead with her to drop it off at school.

What should Mark's mother do?

She became angry and lectured Mark about how inconvenient it was for her and how irresponsible he was. 'You are so careless. Why can't you be organised like your sister?' became Mark's mother's mantra. She would constantly chant this mantra after school, during dinnner, at breakfast and before departing for school. The more mother chanted, the more Mark went into his own adolescent world of thought. His behaviour did not change.

As an adult, mother could have decided that she was being used and abused and that Mark was showing no signs of change. She could sit Mark down and calmly explain the problem to him. She could tell Mark that she was going to give him a present of three calls a year. It was his choice when he used them. Like the TV show 'Who Wants to Be a Millionaire?', once you've used up your chances to get help, you're on your own.

Mark would have to take responsibility for how he chose to use them. If he called his mother, she could say 'You have two calls left for the year, do you want to use one of them now?' Mark would soon learn to choose, and sometimes decline, accepting the consequences of his decision to forget whatever it was that should have been brought to school.

The problem with being a rescuer

Is there a problem with this pervasive rescuing behaviour by parents? Absolutely! These parents are denying their children the opportunity to learn from the consequences of their behaviour. The generation of parents before them set down guidelines and boundaries. Perhaps they were guilty of telling their children what to do and what not to do. The thing they got right was permitting their children to accept the consequences of what they did. If you got into trouble at school and complained to your parents, you would get into more trouble at home. You learned to be quiet, accept the reality of your ways, and to think about what you might to choose to do in the future.

CASE STUDY: A helping handicap

A young man had achieved sufficiently well in his last year of school to win a part-scholarship to university. He was the toast of his family and school. In the first semester he enjoyed university life and failed to meet the level needed to maintain his scholarship. By the grace of the dean of the faculty in which he was studying, he was permitted to maintain his scholarship into second semester. The condition was that he would perform at the appropriate level. Second semester finished with an equally dismal performance.

A review of the student's status revealed that his success at upper secondary level had been the result of more than a fair share of help from his parents, who had spoon-fed him through his final years. Much of his assessable work appeared to have been written by his parents and others. His scholarship was revoked and he left the university.

These parents deluded themselves. As adults they would appreciate that they had removed the responsibility from the child. They created dependence on themselves and taught their son that if something was difficult or he didn't want to do it, he could escape or avoid the task – someone else would pick up the responsibility. But at university, no-one was going to do his work for him. Independence in the child, in this case, was sadly missing.

How common is this parental behaviour? Just look at the statistics throughout Australia for the dropout rate from university by first-year students who have come straight from school. Between 15 and 25 per cent of first-year university students, coming straight from school, fail to satisfactorily complete their year. I do acknowledge that some first-year university students may have selected inappropriate courses, but this is most likely to be a minority group amongst those who fail to complete first year at university.

Let's assume for the moment that you would like your child to go on to study at a tertiary institution one day. Let's consider the skill set needed by a student to perform satisfactorily at first-year tertiary level. The student needs to:

- choose to attend lectures, tutorials and lab classes as no-one is going to chase them
- take full responsibility for their own time management
- be equipped to handle a freer social environment that will expose them to the use of alcohol and drugs
- be able to find their own solutions to problems as there will be minimal extra teacher support
- network with fellow students in order to meet his or her needs
- be creative and adept at finding the information they need – research skills are critical
- be able to cope with a sense of isolation and rely on themselves until new networks are formed
- develop an independent and critical style of thinking
- be responsible for their money management.

Over-supported, propped-up students who have had parents running around after them tend to fail. Placed in a tertiary environment where they have to accept full responsibility for their learning behaviour, these students tend to fall over like a pack of cards.

How easy it is for a parent to unwittingly teach a child to develop a set of behaviours which are compatible with dependence. For example, look again at these words:

- removal of responsibility
- dependence
- avoidance
- escape

They describe neatly some of the characteristic features of drug and alcohol dependence. Interesting! And yet we would ask: 'Why does my child take drugs?' It makes no sense – or does it?

But sadly, we often don't see the effects of what we do. This is not a question of blaming the parents. It is not our role to judge others. It is just very sad that so many parents operate on 'automatic pilot' without any clear rationale to guide them.

Remember: children need to learn that there are outcomes from decisions that they make independently. Decision-making is a skill that is necessary for success in adult life.

CASE STUDY: The disobedient son

Hussan migrated to Australia in the late 1980s. He had come from the Middle East with his wife Yassim and had found it very hard to gain employment. He worked as a factory hand until he had an industrial accident in the mid-1990s, when he damaged the nerves in his hand. He could no longer work and had to be content trying to bring up the family on social welfare payments. He was a proud and sad man.

Ali was his eldest boy and was studying at university. He met Simone, a fellow student, and fell madly in love with her. The problem was that she was Christian and Ali was Muslim. Religion was no issue to Simone and Ali. Physical attraction was more powerful.

However, their families had different views. Simone's brothers were very protective of her and aggressive in their attitude to Ali. Hussan could not suffer the indignity of a disobedient and disloyal son. This was the final straw that broke the camel's back. Loss of job, loss of income, suffering as a migrant and now his eldest son having a mind of his own and rejecting family values. Hussan and Ali argued vigorously about Simone and Ali fell very ill. He was diagnosed as suffering from a major medical condition brought about by stress. His physical state had been brought about by stress. Ali decided that the relationship wasn't worth the price he was paying and broke off with Simone.

Ali made his own decision but under significant pressure from others. The sad outcome was ongoing poor health which led to the need to defer his university course. At the time of writing, he had not returned to university studies. Perhaps he may do so in the future.

Controlling Our Egos

Sometimes, we need to put our own egos on hold and let our children make mistakes from which they can learn. By being strongly focused on our role as parent, we can easily lose focus on what the child needs in order to develop. Learning occurs when the child has to make connections in his or her mind between pieces of experience. As adults, we can discriminate between an error that is safe and one that might constitute a danger to children. Permitting someone to light matches near petrol may be the final learning experience that occurs!

An ego is a sense of identity. It is how we see ourselves and the confidence that we express in our knowledge of who we are. Having children contributes to our sense of self. However, using our children to unhealthily boost our sense of self is denying them the opportunity to grow. The embarrassment that can arise from a child getting into trouble need not occur if we remain secure in ourselves as adults.

If you don't feel secure, remember this slogan:

Fake it till you make it.

In other words, don't let your own insecurity be so transparent to your children that they feed off your insecurity.

Some parents, either believing that they need to be totally honest with their children or lacking self-insight, expose all their worries and concerns to their children. They will constantly talk about how worried or troubled they are about a situation. The expression of concern is rarely accompanied by solutions. They creatively paint a portrait of an adult who is lacking control of their circumstances, driven by fear and a nervous wreck.

How would you like to grow up with a parent like that? It would be a fairly irritating, and potentially very unsettling, experience. Frankly, such parents would be better advised to work on themselves rather than projecting their emotional garbage on to those around them!

CASE STUDY: Too much nagging

Douglas had won a scholarship to a leading Sydney private school. His single mother,

Nancy, was troubled by his irregular attendance, lack of homework and general dis-courtesy to herself and his sister Annie. Nancy would wake him up three or four times each morning, drive him to school as he was always late, and constantly nag him about homework and responsibility. Tensions grew within the home. Little agreement was achieved on anything, and Douglas was demanding his share of his mother's pension and Youth Allowance so that he could move out of home. After sitting with mother and son for ninety minutes, their counsellor hardly said a word except to greet and farewell them. Mother sobbed for most of the session and in an agitated state shared all her concerns about her son directly to the counsellor. Douglas in return, became louder and louder in his attempt to get his mother to listen. Typically of an adolescent, his patience evaporated and he leapt from his chair and showered his mother with every four-letter word and expletive that he could muster. Two days later, Douglas moved out of home and sought refuge with friends. A few weeks later his scholarship was withdrawn by the school and Douglas lost his membership of that school community.

Douglas is at risk of not completing his secondary education at this stage of his life. Most of his time is taken up by a preoccupation with emotional traumas. He is not clear-headed enough to focus his energy on his studies. He lacks a number of the key ingredients for success, in particular:

- the ability to see the connection between the decisions he makes and the outcomes of those decisions
- the capacity to be responsible for his own behaviour, as his mother has unwittingly created a dependent, unthinking child.

Adults Visualise a Positive Outcome

As we become more comfortable with our adult sense of identity, we become more confident about the future.

Whatever your mind can conceive and believe your mind can achieve.

—Napoleon Hill

At all times visualise your children being successful. Never let the pic-ture fade from your conscious mind. Letting go of your picture will allow fear, doubt and negativity to grab you. Once these take hold of your mind, your behaviour towards your children will deteriorate. You will become as despondent as they are. Interestingly, even though children don't verbalise it, they do look to their parents for optimism and confidence that things will be better in the future.

Adults accept the reality that there are unexpected and uncontrolled events in life that may affect people's lives: accidents, illnesses, collapses of the economy. Look beyond external events that impact on your children's lives. Maintain your vision of your child coping with life's demands and being successful. Failure to set a goal, in any area of life, may result in poor outcomes. Raising children is no exception. Whilst there is life, there is hope!

It's Their Life, Not Ours

It should be clear that helping children to do something because they have asked for some support is perfectly legitimate. They have learnt the skill of seeking assistance if they need it. Our task is to learn the difference between a child seeking appropriate support and a child who is transferring their responsibility to their parent.

Choosing, as an adult, to take on the responsibility that belongs to the child leads to problems. An example of this is an adult who lacks confidence in their child's judgement and abilities and therefore takes responsibility onto themselves. The child feels betrayed and is more likely to behave immaturely, as the parent expected. The parent blames the child for being 'worthless' and uses this an excuse to continue their control over the child.

CASE STUDY: Call us if you need us

Rachael had never found mathematics easy. Her school careers advisor had suggested to her that she take one of the harder mathematics courses in her last year at school so that she would qualify for entry to the university course to which she aspired. Her parents had told her at the start of her final year at school that she must take responsibility for her work performance, and that they did not intend to intrude on her studies. They invited her to ask for help or support as she felt she needed it. It was clearly stated that Rachael must initiate the request.

Her parents stood back and allowed Rachael, by trial and error, to learn that she was at risk of failing the subject. How tempting it could have been for her parents to step in after the first term report. They resisted the temptation. Her parents simply reminded her of her goal. In her own time, Rachael asked her parents to obtain some tutoring, and her final scores in a subject that she disliked were good enough: she qualified for her university course. After the year was over, her parents remarked on how stress-free it had been for the whole family. They enjoyed each others' company and continued a good adult relationship with each other.

As adults, Rachael's parents had chosen to recognise that they were not doing the final year at school. They had done that themselves many years before, so why would they choose to become stressed by it again? Choosing not to absorb other people's stress is a key skill. They were comfortable with the thought that if Rachael didn't achieve her first goal of gaining a place in her desired university course, then she would have to review her goal.

'But what happens if they don't do well at school?' many parents have asked me. I can hear the fear in their voices as they imagine their child in some unrewarding work or, at worst, unemployed. Fear in this situation, as I suggested earlier, is not a positive motivator. You are likely to take actions in response to the fear rather than in the best interests of the child's learning and growing. My usual response is: 'Help them to see that it is *their* responsibility to gain something from the education process.'

As an adult, you need to enable your child to discover the purpose. Parents usually feel very uncomfortable doing this because not being protective of the child is too much of a risk. 'What if they fail?' parents ask me. The answer is fairly obvious – they will learn from the outcome of their decision. The adult response is to keep alive the mental picture of your child being successful. Never let go of that picture. It may just take a little longer for them to experience success.

Education Is Our Children's Business

Ultimately, the child needs to identify and accept the value of education. If they don't, then that becomes their issue. They have to live with the consequence. If they have made the wrong choice about commitment to learning, a couple of years in a repetitive job will be a strong motivator for them to return to learning. If they don't pursue further learning, then they probably would never have done well anyway and that's a reality.

Just keep visualising your child as a successful adult. Many an adult has experienced success without participating fully in education.

CASE STUDY: A second chance

Joanne had left school at the end of Year 11. Her father was an abusive alcoholic and her mother expertly played the victim role. The emotional hothouse of the family home was not conducive, particularly if you were female, to continuing education. Encouragement and opportunity were lacking.

Joanne obtained a position at the local Safeway store and found achievement and dignity in the job. She felt proud of her capacity to make independent financial decisions. After a few months of work, Joanne decided to move from her home town to the city, and took up a management traineeship with a fast-food chain. After two years with them, she had learnt that she was a quick learner, a good time manager and competent in what she did. 'Why not return to education?' she thought. Joanne had always had an interest in criminology. She located a TAFE course which interested her, and after twelve months of study, she was so encouraged by her results that she made a decision to undertake a university degree, on a part-time basis, upon completion of her present course.

For Joanne, the value of education was only visible after she had removed herself from the direct influence of her parents. It was as a result of her experiences in the workforce, not her parents' attitude, that she discovered her intelligence.

As an adult, be clear on why your child doesn't embrace education. There can be a variety of causes, not the least of which is the nature of the domestic environment, as exemplified by Joanne's case. However, there can be other causes that are unrelated to the role that parents play in their children's lives.

Learning Difficulties

A child who is frustrated and bored at school may have an underlying difficulty with learning or memory. Be alert, as an adult to the possibility of some form of learning problem. Seek appropriate professional assistance if your child continually struggles with his or her learning.

Your child's lack of performance may be caused by something other than attitude. Seek clear information and guidance from your school about your child's performance. If you are not satisfied with the response you receive from the school, seek external assistance through a psychologist who specialises in learning (see Where Can I Get Help on page 143).

If a child has a physical handicap or other specific disability that affects learning and this is the most likely reason that they are not doing well at school, then encourage the child to work with you to seek help and support. This would be an adult response. Talk to your child about the benefits of finding out what is wrong and relieving their (and your) worry. This will help the child to deal with reality.

Reality's Okay

'Reality' is a word many parents avoid, particularly those parents who are into 'rescuing' their children. Mature adults accept the word but parents will often want to protect their children from reality. This is most likely to arise from parental fear of the consequences of permitting their children to make a decision. Parents are uncomfortable with the risk.

Reality means that none of us are perfect all day. Reality means that we do sometimes become tired, ill and despondent. Reality means that we sometimes fail to meet our own expectations and those of others. Reality means that we sometimes fail. And children are no exception. Reality affects them.

The idea that 'Reality is fine as long as it doesn't affect my child' is rarely articulated, but an examination of the actions of parents will show that this belief often underlies their own behaviour.

CASE STUDY: Clear thinking went up in smoke

Hamish was a senior student at a very well respected school. He started experimenting with marijuana at 14 years of age. By 16 he had become dependent. The only way he could get through a day at school was to smoke a couple of joints before school and at lunch hour. His motivation to learn deteriorated and his academic performance declined. More and more days were spent being absent from school as a result of his regular use of marijuana, which was combined with alcohol and regular partying. In family sessions, his father would vigorously try to persuade Hamish to abandon his habit.

When asked by his therapist how Hamish financially supported his extensive use of marijuana and alcohol, he replied 'My father gives me the money for it.' Father confirmed that this was true and stated that his reason was to save the family the embarrassment of having his son engage in criminal activity to support his habit.

Father was not a stupid man, but how easily he had slipped off his adult hat and put on his parent hat!

Parents focus on being protective. Their aim is to protect the child from the reality of the outcomes that result from a lack of work, commitment and habits. The motive is pure, but the technique creates the opposite effect to that which is desired. The price to be paid is substantial for everyone concerned. In the above example, Hamish was not facing his drug use and its effect upon him. His parents were embarrassed and upset by the consequences of a potential

criminal charge. Unwittingly, they were encouraging his dependence.

I suggested in Chapter 1 that adults are the guardians of reality. This is a very special responsibility for adults. If they choose to relinquish it, we are at risk of having a society that is increasingly dysfunctional.

Are You A Robber?

If you do too much for your children, you will rob them of motivation to perform and achieve. In addition, you run the risk of having them lose respect for you.

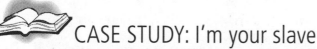

CASE STUDY: I'm your slave

Lindy and George had four children. They believed that their role as parents was to provide their children with every opportunity. George held a senior position in the advertising industry and was financially successful, but their decision to put four children through private school created financial pressure. There was an annual school fees bill in excess of $50,000, and a mortgage on the larger house they had moved to so that each child could have their own bedroom. Increasing personal loans, credit cards and bank overdrafts kept the family afloat.

Lindy was a dedicated mother. She prepared meals and snacks on demand and provided a taxi service for all four children on command. Every morning Lindy would wake each child to get ready for school. She would be greeted with various forms of abuse as she rushed between bedrooms, kitchen and bathroom. By the fourth wake-up call for each child she would become a little jaded and despondent; such early-morning greetings as 'go away bitch' and 'f*** off' did little to build her self-esteem. Not infrequently her children would remind her that she was a 'bludger' because she didn't have a real job like their father.

Each day, Lindy would remind herself that it was all worthwhile. She and George were giving the children the best chance in life. Ski trips, holidays to Club Med, clothing and entertainment ensured that the children 'gained the best opportunities' as Lindy and George grew older and sank into a quagmire of debt.

Life was beautiful until the day Lindy walked out, in an attempt to re-establish her sense of self and meaning.

Not only was Lindy and George's relationship being sorely tested, but the four children had grown into young adults who were self-centred and demanding, and held little respect for their parents. The children eagerly looked forward to Lindy and George's demise and the possibility of a shared inheritance in order to maintain their self-indulgent lifestyle. Little did they know the real financial position of their parents and the size of the debt. Reality, in the future, was going to hit home hard.

> *The richest heritage a young man can have is to be born into poverty.*
>
> —Andrew Carnegie

Andrew Carnegie is credited with creating America's steel industry. He arrived in America as a poor immigrant Scottish boy. He saw his own humble start to life not as a deterrent to success, but as an inspiration to overcome obstacles and achieve goals. Carnegie was not only successful as an industrialist but as a human being. By the time of his death in 1919 he had given away US$350 million towards helping people. Imagine what that sum could be today!

Finding the balance between inspiring your children to achieve and robbing them of incentive is the challenge for you as the adult.

Now link this to decision-making. How often do your children say to you 'I need ...'? Out of guilt and a sense of convenience to self, it is often easy for the parent to say to their child: 'Next time we are out shopping, darling, we will get it.'

How would an adult handle such a request? Keep in mind, it is not the specific item that's being asked for that's the issue, but the reality that someone has to earn the money in order to provide it. If the item is not absolutely essential, the adult might reply: 'Great idea, darling. I will go halves. You put in half the cost and I will match it.' Nothing is a better test of how essential an item is to an individual. Wait for the response and you will know!

Communication: Keeping It Simple

Children and adolescents in particular develop an allergy to *adult-talk* and *parent-talk*. Step into a child's shoes and look from the child's point of view; their entire world is filled with adults who constantly talk *at* them. Each and every living moment of the day, at home and in every classroom, there is an adult demanding that they be listened to. The result: the child gets an overdose of adult talk. Watch your child's eyes glaze over as you engage them in a conversation. For many parents, a conversation is actually synonymous with a monologue.

Parents start talking and demand that the child listen. Provided that the child occasionally says 'nah', 'yeah' and 'don't know' as the parent continues to talk at them, the parent believes that they have an audience and the child is concentrating on what is being said.

Yet, interestingly, who becomes the most frustrated with the lack of engagement? It's the parent: 'I don't know why I talk to you, you never listen or say anything intelligent. It's like talking to a wall.' We are so often very quick to place the responsibility on to the child. We judge them, from our perspective, as being immature, uncooperative, moody, sullen, withdrawn and a problem. Alas, this is rarely true. We are the ones with the problem. We have failed to understand that our children engage with information in a different way from us, and that they are fatigued by the constant and continuing demand that they spend their lives listening to adult talk.

We know from our life experience that people who are fearful or anxious tend to speed up the pace of their speech. They also tend to have difficulty succinctly expressing their thoughts – the right words seem to escape them. As a result, they become very tiring to listen to. It is a major task attempting to gain meaning from their incessant chatter. It is these very same people who are so anxious to tell you why they think that children don't listen to a word that is being said to them. Nor do they pause and reflect on the other person's feelings.

How much time have you spent in getting to know your child? Do you listen to what they think and feel? Their response may not be an adult one but then, after all, they are not adults. No wonder young people congregate in packs and talk to each other. It is not surprising that they consume the largest part of our domestic telephone time and cost in talking with their friends.

I remember one boy saying to me that 'Mum doesn't have a conversation with me. She just tells me how it is. It doesn't matter what I think, I just have to do it her way anyway and she wonders why I switch off.'

How frequently parents engage in this behaviour. Their focus is on telling the child. The pace of their speech reflects their own underlying anxiety, and there is very little real communication. Communication is not a one-way street. A minimum of two participants are needed, unless you are content to talk to a mirror!

Children need to understand or comprehend what we are trying to say. Recognise that children don't learn by uncritically absorbing everything that we say. We might think that what we are saying is terribly important – they may not. Our timing may be wrong.

If children communicate with others, think, discuss and disagree with much of what they hear, they are in fact positively responding to what is being said to them. Talking and debating ideas is a healthy way of learning to assess the value of each idea put to them.

As an adult, develop the skill of engaging your child in discussion and debate. Encourage it by using an appropriate tone of voice. Don't automatically see a challenge to what you have said as the start of an argument. Don't feel threatened that your power will be undermined. We have to be secure enough in ourselves to see the value of what is occurring. Remember our motto:

Fake it till you make it.

Look confident, sound confident and appear like an adult in front of your child.

Taking The Time

Communicating takes time. As parents we are so time-conscious. Often the need to be efficient transcends any consideration of taking the time to listen, to discuss and to reason, to negotiate and to seek cooperation based on a considered understanding of what we are saying. My suspicion is that with families in which there are either two working parents or an employed single parent now being the norm, this problem will be with us for some time to come.

The reality is that in our society many parents work outside the home. A consequence is that each day our children see us in two situations:

- rushing in the morning to get out the door to work
- fatigued and agitated at night trying to organise meals, household tasks and homework.

Opportunities to take time to build a relationship with our children are reduced by the daily demands upon us.

CASE STUDY: Making up her own mind

Megan had been at her present school for only two years. She was dissatisfied with the standard of teaching and the pace of work. She felt that the day went very slowly and that there was much wasted time. Teachers were focused on class discipline and sometimes lost direction in their teaching. It would have been so easy for her parents to tell her to stick it out at this school but they resisted the temptation. Megan was given the opportunity to draw up a list of things that she wanted from a school. After doing so, she was invited to reflect on her goal for post-secondary education and how the next two years at school would affect the achievement of her goal.

Her parents helped her to select two schools that were geographically convenient and met the specifications that she had drawn up. Megan then looked at both schools. The outcome from the process was that Megan chose to stay at her present school. In the next two months her mood was good and she happily went to school each day. She also chose to gain more from her present school by being more actively involved in drama and debating.

Twelve months later, Megan is performing at an A level in all her subjects, enjoys a good relationship with both parents and is planning her final secondary school studies with enthusiasm.

Enabling Megan to make up her own mind was a time-consuming process for her parents. Yet the long-term gain will be enormous. Here is a young woman who, at age 16, has learnt to understand her own needs and how to respond responsibly to what is happening in her life. It would have been quicker and more convenient for her parents to say: 'No. Stay where you are and stop complaining.' But at what cost? The time they invested in allowing her to work through the process was an investment in Megan becoming a responsible young adult.

It does take time to use these opportunities for the child to learn. Busy parents often don't have the time or can't see beyond the task to use it to the child's advantage. There is no shortcut! We need to be sensitive to the fact that in order to bring up a child to be a responsible young adult, time is going to be needed. 'Quality time' is an expression frequently used by parents to describe the minimal interaction they have with their children. Adults recognise it as a rationalisation, i.e. a plausible-sounding excuse for *not* spending time with children. Rationalisations help parents to temporarily dampen their feelings of guilt.

Children will differ in the amount of time they need from their parents. Their needs will vary, depending on what is happening in their life at a given time. Involvement in your child's life means time. The time you spend playing, listening, conversing and encouraging their interests is critical to a child's development. For a child to grow up feeling secure and confident, consistency of involvement by a parent–adult in their life is essential. Consistency of time spent in a child's life also provides a relationship in which the child will be less resentful of a parent if a disciplinary issue arises. Children are more willing to acknowledge or accept the view of a parent with whom they have had time to develop a relationship.

We should be aware that the amount of time that we choose to give or not to give to our children may have an effect on the development of their ability to learn. A lack of time spent with them will also have an impact on their emotional development. There is plenty of evidence to support these claims.

A recent British National Child Development study found that seven-year-old children of mothers who worked full-time had poorer reading and mathematics grades than children whose mothers worked part-time or were at home.

In a 1986 US Department of Education study, Milne, Myers, Rosenthal and Ginsburg showed that maternal employment was linked to lower mathematics and reading scores. The more the mother worked, the stronger was the effect!

A 1988 California State University study by Gottfried and colleagues found that if a mother worked in excess of 30 hours per week, reading and intellectual ability were affected. Similar findings have been found in a combined Charles Sturt University and Macquarie University study released in Australia in 2000. These studies suggest that some time in the day needs to be allocated to connecting with your child.

These findings are not surprising. Young children need to bond to a parent, not to a childcare worker. Their sense of security has its roots in their needs being met at a young age. If a child enjoys the encouragement that comes from sharing things with a parent, they are more likely to embrace learning. If the child senses that they are an add-on extra in their parents' lives, they are unlikely to trust or communicate deeply with them. Why? The child has learnt, through the example of its parents, that career or other issues are the priority. When that priority has been serviced, the child can then gain space and attention. The research suggests that working parents and single parents need to recognise that as a result of fatigue, their manner and attitude may communicate the wrong message to a child.

We sometimes wonder why teenagers are reluctant to communicate with their parents or other adults. Looking at their early childhood experiences might suggest the reason:

A lack of emotional connection with the younger child leads to an absence of communication in the teenage years.

This is particularly noticeable with separated parents who step in and out of a child's life. Separated parents are frequently surprised by the response or lack thereof that they receive from their child. No wonder. If you are not there at the time your child needs you, then you have missed the opportunity to connect, and distanced the child in the process.

An emotional connection arises from a parent being able to service the emotional needs of a young child at the time the child needs affection or reassurance. Younger children are 'here and now' people who haven't matured sufficiently to delay the satisfaction of their needs.

And remember those lovely grandparents who had the time and motivation to provide a balance to our parents and to listen to how we felt and thought? If your children have positive and active grandparents in their life, both you and they are blessed. Build the relationship between them. Grand parents can be an antidote for many of the things that you may do to your children! They help to create a balance for a child. They are your child's emotional lifeline.

CASE STUDY: A single mum

Richard was an only child. Sadly, his father Andrew was killed in a motor vehicle accident just before Richard's fifth birthday. Helen, his mother, was devastated. In addition to the grief and trauma, there quickly emerged an anxiety about their financial position. Only two weeks before Andrew's death, they had discussed the need to take out an insurance policy, but at when he died, a policy had not yet been arranged.

Helen thought about the mortgage and all the other costs of living and educating Richard. There was no choice. She would need to re-enter the workforce. Sensitive to the needs of Richard, Helen decided to compromise between part-time work as a nurse and spending time with her son. She resolved that when he was well-established in primary school she would consider a full-time position. This, she argued, would allow her to spend time with him. Enabling Richard to come home to his mother rather than to an empty house, reading together and not being too stressed were Helen's goals.

On occasion, Helen's father would help out and babysit or pick up Richard from kindergarten. Her mother had died ten years before Andrew did. All worked fairly well. Like most families, there were tense times. Today, Richard is studying for a BSc degree, having achieved very good secondary school results. He is well adjusted, has an active social life and enjoys a good relationship with his mother. He is planning to move out and share a flat with some university friends.

Other adults can also play a role in your child's life – aunts and uncles or family friends can all provide balance to your role. Life is never black or white. There are different choices that can be made. In Helen's case, she chose to balance her work against her son's emotional and educational needs. She would appear to have struck the right balance for them both, an amazing achievement on Helen's part given the tremendous pressure that she was under.

Choose Your Moment

So am I saying 'Let your children do their own thing' – that we as parents don't have the right to tell them anything? No. There is a time and place to say something. We recognise this principle in our relationships with other adults.

As the adults most involved with them, we need to recognise that our children are saturated in adult talk. We therefore need to make judgements about how and when we are going to say something and at what length we will say it.

If a child is tired and their thoughts are clearly focused elsewhere, a wise adult will recognise that their need to communicate with the child is less important than the child's need for some space.

Teenagers will avoid talking to adults for fear of revealing their vulnerabilities.

They are also typically fearful of adults asking them questions. When you ask a teenager why they avoid communication with a parent, they will often reply that if parents become involved in an issue, a punishment is inevitably around the corner. It is a fear of punitive consequences that often reduces the teenager to silence.

When was the last time you just opened your mouth and said something? We all do it. Often, however, something left unsaid is better than something said. Think first: what do I want say? Why do I want to say it, and how will my child respond if I say it now? Observe your child's mental state: are they tired after their time at school or kindergarten? Are they absorbed in some activity that is meaningful to them? A television show or computer game may not be meaningful to you, but is it something that they value? We know how we feel when our child or a telephone call interrupts us when we are watching our favourite TV show or a video after a long and tiring day. In that respect children are not much different from us. Take time, before you open your mouth, to assess the whole situation. This may be a new skill that you need to develop.

In the current generation of children, spending time on the computer playing games and surfing the Internet are popular. Australia has the highest level of home PC ownership in the Pacific Rim. Many children have their own email addresses and spend time communicating with others through the Internet. This is important time to them. It is a way for them to fulfil their need to develop social relationships with others.

Our needs and our child's needs may clash and if they do, you as the adult will lose. Children are unbelievably powerful in winning in a conflict with a parent. They have a youthful tenacity that can be hard to match. Sometimes your needs can be reconciled by choosing to avoid a power battle with your child. Simply wait – be patient.

CASE STUDY: TV wars

Maxine enjoyed her favourite TV soapies. Each day at school, she and her girlfriends would discuss the plot and drool over the show's sex symbol. They would fantasise about having a boyfriend like Elliot, one of the teenage leads in the show. Failure to see an episode would result in Maxine missing out on participating in lunchtime conversation. It was a little bit like her father's insistence that he saw the football results every Sunday night so that he could discuss the weekend's games and take part in the footy tipping conversation at work on Monday morning.

Yet there was a problem. The TV soapies corresponded with the preparation and eating of the family meal. Maxine's mother had the view that her daughter needed to help at this time of the day instead of lolling about in front of the television. Mother would call, yell and demand that certain things be done right throughout the soapie. Maxine would yell back, and one day in frustration told her Mother to 'f*** off'.

The result? Maxine's mother insisted that the television be confiscated and locked in their bedroom cupboard. Maxine burst into tears and hid in her bedroom for five hours, having barricaded the door with her chest of drawers and refusing to acknowledge the plaintive and muffled pleas of both parents to come out and talk.

How much easier life would have been if her parents had negotiated with Maxine to videotape her favourite program so that she could watch it later in the evening. Instead, the situation became a power battle that Maxine was determined she wasn't going to lose. Next morning, Maxine went to the Student Welfare Coordinator at school to make an application for youth accommodation. After many conferences, Maxine decided to stay at home with her somewhat chastened parents, who were resentful that they had been undermined by the system.

Most adults recognise that there is little value in making judgements about what is of value to another. Some adults like to watch sport on television, others prefer a movie. Others still can't stand TV at all. For Maxine, the television soapie had a value that was not readily perceived or understood by her parents.

Develop a sensitivity to your child's needs and personal space. Switching off and daydreaming in childhood and adolescence has its adult counterparts in relaxing and meditating.

One young student commented to me the other week 'How do you think I feel? I walk in the back door after school and the first thing my Mum says to me is "What have you got for homework?" She can get stuffed.' I tend to agree. Mother stuffed as an ornament would be of higher value than her behaviour and lack of awareness at the moment. But there is good news. Mum has seen the light and is choosing to change, much to her own joy and her daughter's relief. Mother and daughter have agreed to talk about topics other than school. The bond between mother and daughter can be built on more interesting things.

You can choose to maintain the view that you are the parent and therefore have both a responsibility and a right to tell your child whatever it is that you want to tell them. You are also choosing to have the same problems recur that might be troubling you now. Does this sound like a familiar formula? If you are the type of parent who repeatedly tells your child something – keep going, they'll grow up one day, move out of home and then you might be happy. You can entertain yourself, in their absence, with the question 'I wonder why they never listened to me?'

To Nag Or Not to Nag?

One day you might find yourself yelling at your child and the next day you try to stay calm. You promise yourself that you will never nag again, yet two days later the child has been asked to do something for the fifteenth time. What do you do? You can feel guilty and despondent. Finally, exhausted, you may form the view that it doesn't really matter anyway. Whatever is done and however it is done, the child doesn't change their behaviour! The child blithely wanders along with the same attitudes and bad habits, as if they were oblivious to your existence.

This happens because the child isn't clear about exactly what will happen when he or she misbehaves. Your child is not getting clear instructions on what sort of behaviour will produce what response. If this situation continues, the child will become increasingly insecure, and this will lead to worse behaviour still.

Here are three tips to remember when attempting to make changes:

- If you repeat yourself and nag your child, you are training the child to become dependent on you.
- Negativity breeds contempt. The word 'No' should be used sparingly. Only use the word 'No' for situations that involve safety or those situations that really are non-negotiable.
- Constant change in disciplining children creates chaos and confusion.

Whatever you do, don't expect instant change. Just as the medication you receive from a doctor takes time to cure you, so too will any steps you take to improve your child's behaviour.

You are also more likely to be patient and continue to use a technique if you understand the reasons for using it. Observe your child's behaviour. You need to discover how you may be acting as a trigger to the bad behaviour that you see.

Don't be a nag: constant repetition of an instruction undermines our children's belief in our parenting ability. This then leads to the belief that they do not need to act until our request is accompanied by threats of injury and death uttered in a loud and confronting voice. Instead of thinking for themselves and taking responsibility for doing things, they become dependent on constant reminders to trigger them into action.

And don't despair – change is possible. Permanent change is *definitely* possible. Yes, that's right, permanent change in a child's behaviour *is* possible. I have seen extraordinary changes many times in my own work.

CASE STUDY: Keeping to your game plan

Mark was a lively child. Some people had described him as hyperactive. His Grade 5 teacher suspected that he was suffering from attention deficit disorder (ADD). Grandma believed that he was poorly raised by his parents, who seemed to her to be unable to effectively discipline him.

Mark's household was full of shouting and yelling. He would run wildly around the house pursued by an angry and screaming parent. The more Mark yelled and swore, the louder both his parents became. It was rare for anyone in the house to have a conversation in a normal tone or at normal volume.

By age 11, Mark had been threatened with a shortened lifespan, locked in his room, had his Nintendo confiscated and was banned from having friends come to stay. But nothing changed. Mark continued the behavioural pattern and his parents became more despairing in their loss of confidence. He had reduced them to nervous, insecure and unhappy people. They had tried everything to change his behaviour, including a request to their family medical practitioner to put either him or themselves on medication!

In the course of therapy, the focus shifted from trying to change Mark to teaching his parents to change. What could they do differently? They learned that as Mark raised his voice and became more physically active, they could move in the opposite direction. They learned the skill of lowering the volume of their voice, slowing down their pace of speech and developing an unemotional and almost flat tone to their voice.

What happened? Initially, things became worse, probably because Mark didn't believe that he wasn't getting the same response that he had always gained. Yet courageously his parents maintained their composure and focused on changing how they responded to him. They smiled if he was good and they had a blank face if he wasn't. After two weeks, change was evident. After four weeks, the situation had stabilised. By six weeks, Mark was a changed child. For the first time in years, things seemed relatively normal.

But what if your child is a teenager? Can teenagers change or is it too late? Well, it's definitely harder to influence a child's behaviour after puberty, but it is most certainly possible.

With teenagers, you will need to focus on key behaviours that you would like to see change. You will need to turn a blind eye to relatively unimportant things like haircuts or the cleanliness of their bedroom, and focus on behaviours that have more serious consequences, such as attitudes at school, or relationships with boyfriends or girlfriends. Negotiate with your teenager. Revisit Chapter 4 and familarise yourself with the process. Agree on consequences and quietly remain constant in your approach. A child who is unused to making decisions will need time to adjust to a new way of interacting with their parents.

Is It Worth Saying?

Think very carefully before you open your mouth. Check what you are going to say:

- Do I have my adult hat on?
- Is the statement I am about to make absolutely critical to this child's wellbeing?
- Is the issue that I am about to comment on of major importance to me and the family?
- Am I about to launch into a lengthy explanation on some issue?
- How can I use this experience to teach my child about decision-making and responsibility?

Think about this:

The parent who says less is frequently the parent who is more listened to by the child.

On talkback radio, silence is used to maximum effect. A pause in the host's speech before a key point is made will heighten listeners' attentiveness to what is being said. Apply this principle in your daily communication.

Throw away the belief that you have to open your mouth and comment on everything that the child does or doesn't do. You will frequently find that by saying nothing, you will eliminate an undesirable behaviour more quickly than by actually commenting on it.

The popular belief is that to ignore an inappropriate behaviour is to strengthen the likelihood of its reoccurrence. However, the psychological principle of ignoring the behaviours you don't want to see has much to recommend it. Give the child your attention when there are behaviours that you would like to see occur more frequently.

CASE STUDY: Rude kid

Joel was your classic attention-seeking younger sibling who was overshadowed by three older sisters. Joel had learnt, by nine years of age, that doing something dramatic was a guaranteed way of having attention focused on him. His favourite technique for achieving his goal was to use language that caused his parents and grandmother to express the desire to 'wash his mouth out with soap'. This was an old fashioned cure applied to children who used bad language in an attempt to cure them of the habit.

Each time Joel uttered a four-letter word, conversation would cease, Joel would jump up and down with glee, and threats of punishment would flow from his parents. Grandmother would use these opportunities to repeat parts of one of her dearly departed husband's sermons on godliness. Joel would smirk and this would further infuriate those present. The more Joel's audience responded, the more Joel performed.

In this case, attention could have been better directed towards Joel when he was not being outrageous. By ignoring Joel's behaviour and continuing on as if nothing had occurred, the family would have sent a clear message to him that he could expect to gain little attention by doing what he was doing. To achieve this, a discussion between the adults, in Joel's absence, might have led to a united front.

A Family Conference

The frenetic life that many families live often reduces the amount of time that all family members have in the one place at the one time. Frequently, families eat their evening meal in relays depending on the commitments that the members have. If parents or the single parent work outside the home, attention is often directed towards the practicalities of cooking, cleaning and washing upon returning home. If children have outside school activities in sport, drama or music, practice times will occur during the late afternoon or early evening. The result of this lifestyle is reduced contact and conversation with each other. Issues become inconveniences. Things are poorly thought through. Decisions are rushed. The resulting absence of focused conversation can provide opportunities for problem behaviours to develop.

Sitting and talking together can help to focus all family members on an issue. A family conference can be used to explore issues that affect any family member. Such a conference enables a process to take place, one from which children can learn much. They learn that:

- their needs are important
- they will be listened to
- it is important to listen to and acknowledge the needs of others.

They also develop the skill of expressing what they think and feel, and are exposed to strategies for solving problems and making decisions.

A family conference is simple to run. Here are some guidelines:

- Switch off the television, computer and video.
- Take the phone off the hook or put on the voicemail.
- Sit around a table. (This gives everyone equal status and eye contact.)
- One person talks and the others listen.
- Avoid judging others. Let each person express themselves and what they feel.
- Get a clear picture of the issue.
- Be honest about each other's needs.
- Keep summarising as you go in order to maintain clarity.
- Agree on an outcome. Sometimes both parents and children need to compromise.
- Keep it short.
- At the end, make a statement about the agreed outcome so that everyone is clear.

Family conferences are a useful tool if they are not used too frequently – once a month or so would probably be the right frequency. Otherwise, children may perceive it as a vicious attempt to take their time away from other activities.

The following section further develops the idea of a family conference with reference to the very difficult issue of dealing with violent children.

Violence and its reduction through a family conference

Violence on the part of children and adolescents is becoming more exposed in the media. What causes someone to punch, kick, stab or fire a gun at someone else or even themselves? According to the American Psychological Association, there is no simple answer. Six factors have been identified by them as contributing to violent behaviour:

- Violence can result from a child's inability to release or express feelings of anger or frustration in a healthy way.
- Violence is a way of manipulating others to gain an advantage.
- Violence is a way of retaliating against those who have hurt them.
- Violence is learned behaviour.
- Violence can be used to gain respect or attention.
- Violence is often chosen by those who have low self-worth.

Reflect on your role as an adult and your interaction with your child. Approaches that will minimise the need for expressions of violence include:

- finding healthy means of expressing anger or frustration
- developing positive ways of obtaining advantages within relationships
- obtaining respect and attention from others
- providing opportunities to develop a strong sense of self-worth.

In addition to the other positive things that you do as an adult with your children, a family conference gives an opportunity to strengthen each of these areas. The process of a family conference enables individuals to be listened to and accorded the dignity of expressing their thoughts and feelings, and allows a verbal release for frustration and acknowledgement of self worth. A family conference has both immediate and long-term benefits.

Focus On the Good Behaviour

It is highly unlikely that even the naughtiest or most poorly behaved child is that way 24 hours a day, 365 days a year. It just seems that way to parents who have become totally focused on poor behaviour and lost sight of all the other reasonable and positive things that their child does.

Notice the good things that your child does. These may only be little things. Comment briefly and positively on them. Thank them. Smile at them. Hug them. Give the child your attention for the behaviours that you would like to see occur more frequently. Cultivate the positive 'throw away line'. This is an effective way of acknowledging the good behaviour.

The exception to the rule is when a major safety issue arises. Clearly, if the child is about to run in front of a car, saying something to them is desirable! Let common sense prevail.

CASE STUDY: A homework routine

Sidhu was reluctant to do homework. Each night, he would procrastinate. Television, phone calls and computer games became the first priority when he arrived home. Sidhu's mother, frustrated by his lack of planning and irresponsibility, would gently wail and moan as she prepared the evening meal. She gnashed her teeth in anguish at her son's slothfulness. A recent parent–teacher meeting had reinforced the message that Sidhu was not doing sufficient homework or handing in assignments on time.

Frustration and fear of the consequences of Sidhu's behaviour drove his mother to seek support. She rang the Australian Psychological Society's referral service and obtained the details and telephone number of an educational psychologist. (The details of this service are listed on page 143.)

The psychologist tested Sidhu and found that he had no particular learning problem. Over a couple of sessions the psychologist worked with the mother to develop a technique to train Sidhu to increase his work output at home. This involved two strategies. One was to provide Sidhu with rewards for working. The other was to train his mother to comment positively and briefly on her observations of Sidhu being involved with his schoolwork. Each night, Sidhu was offered computer and television time upon completion of his homework tasks. While he was actually doing his homework, Mother would briefly and positively comment on his behaviour as she passed his bedroom door: 'Oh, you are working so well', she would happily call out to him. Within four weeks, Sidhu had established a new and effective routine. He was more communicative with his parents and happier.

Interestingly, many parents do not realise that by speaking to a child they are giving the child their attention. Children love attention. Naughty or undesirable behaviour is rewarded by the giving of parental attention. What you succeed in doing is encouraging the child, who has a natural desire to gain the attention of their parent, to engage in inappropriate or undesirable behaviour again. 'Aha,' the child says to themselves, 'If I say "Crap" again, I'll get Daddy's attention.' The child is smart. He or she has learnt the connection between engaging in certain behaviours and obtaining parental attention. Inevitably, they will use it to their advantage. Mum and Dad are left wondering why the child is wandering around the house using the word with increasing frequency. The answer is, because they have trained the child to do it by making a constant fuss about the word and its use.

It would be appropriate in these circumstances to choose a time to explain to the child that the use of such words was inappropriate behaviour. Unemotionally explain to the child that such language can cause offence, and that using these words is unlikely to build positive relationships with people.

Children hate being ignored and they will go to extraordinary lengths to be noticed. Contrary to popular belief, even teenagers hate being ignored. They like to be included in the family. A teenager who seeks privacy is not necessarily requesting to be ignored. So often, the need for quiet and private time is misinterpreted by the family as meaning that they do not want to be included. They do want to be included but in a slightly different way to younger children.

Teenagers are busy people. They need time and space to develop their independence, sexual identity and future role in society. The loving family acknowledges their needs and provides a world in which the teenager can simultaneously free themselves from their parents and gain love and support.

So be smart. Keep it simple. Develop an awareness of what you talk about, or comment on, and the effect of what you say on your child. Remember:

The parent who says little has more power. The power of example is often more influential than the words that are spoken.

Children do not learn by being told things. They learn by observing the key adults in their lives. Model in your everyday life the behaviour that you would like to see in your child: honesty, courtesy and respect for others. Children learn from adult explanations, a comprehension of boundaries and the opportunity to learn how to explore choices and predict the outcomes of those choices. And they learn, from experience, that some behaviours will gain them appropriate adult attention and some behaviours are likely to exclude them from the attention that they desire and need.

Put In The Positives

As adults, we are in a powerful position to provide encouragement to our children. All human beings need encouragement in order to grow into positive and competent people. Our self-esteem is closely connected to the type of messages that we receive about ourselves. By choosing our words wisely, we can be of tremendous assistance in building our child's self-esteem.

CASE STUDY: Treated like a queen

Narelle was an attractive, intelligent and charismatic 15-year-old. She had just dropped out of school after becoming frustrated with her schoolwork and teachers. Her relationship with her father had always been difficult. He was very negative in his comments to her. She was constantly told that she was irresponsible, a loser, an idiot.

Narelle had an 18-year-old boyfriend who was heavily involved in the drug scene. When asked why she was so attracted to him, she replied: 'He treats me like a queen.' Therein lay the bond. She felt different about herself when she was with him. She felt important, accepted and attractive. At home she felt like a victim. Her two older sisters were critical of her behaviour. Her father told her she was a loser. She reluctantly believed what she was told. At 15 years of age, she had come to the belief was that she was no good at anything and therefore that there was no point in trying. She expressed her belief by doing nothing all day except see her boyfriend, and constantly complaining that everything was 'boring'.

Narelle *was* a victim – of incessant parental judgement.

Speaking For the Child

Another common parental behaviour is speaking on behalf of a child. You can see this occur in a variety of situations: in doctor's surgeries, parent–teacher interviews, professional consultations, shopping centres, sporting functions and social situations. An adult speaks to a child and their parent answers. When you question the parent about why they engage in this behaviour, they usually reply that they are trying to be helpful. Often the parent is fearful that the child will omit some key piece of information. The child is deprived of an opportunity to think and to frame a response to a question. They sit there mute, brain-dead in the knowledge that there is no need for them to crank up their neurons, because their parent will take over!

CASE STUDY: Mum knows best

Grandma and Grandpa rarely visited their daughter and her family because upon retirement they had retreated to the Gold Coast to avoid the burden of babysitting duties. Each year they would purchase a discount pay-in-advance airfare and do the circuit of their children in Adelaide and Melbourne, showering the grandchildren with chocolates and kisses.

Simone and Peter were always pleased to see their grandparents, and Mary would cook a special meal on the evening that her parents arrived to stay. Trevor, the son-in-law, always insisted on a family meal to welcome the in-laws. Down they sat to a gourmet Indian curry and barbecued sausages for the children.

'How's school, Simone?' Grandma asked.

Simone glanced at her Mother.

'She's doing so well this year with her new teacher,' replied Mary, and so the conversation continued between Grandma and Mary, while Simone munched her barbecued sausages.

Just before retiring, after the children had been tucked up in bed, Grandma took her daughter aside and softly said 'Simone doesn't say much, dear.'

'No Mum, she doesn't. She's very shy,' Mary replied.

They all slept well.

Her mother's desire, as a parent, to keep control and her impatience have stifled Simone's ability to express herself. The consequence of this is that Simone will not develop her personal confidence in expressing what she thinks or feels. This is likely to lead to feelings of inadequacy, and may place Simone in a vulnerable position with her peers.

Sibling Fights

A common feature of family life is the fighting between brothers and sisters. The children work out a pecking order and decide who has power. Each child wrestles with their own position within the family. Power battles emerge. Who is the strongest? Who has control? It is very easy, as a parent, to fall into the role of sorting out disputes over toys, the use of a video game, television and space, but caution needs to be exercised.

CASE STUDY: The usual suspect

Therese had two older sisters. They were all very articulate children. Frequently there would be disputes over entry to bedrooms and toys. Each day their mother would be drawn into a dispute and be asked, by one of the children, to enter judgement upon the guilty party. Mother would jump into the disputes in an effort to put an end to them. She would tell the children that they were 'pathetic and childish' and that she was 'fed up with the constant arguments and squabbles.' On some occasions she would confiscate the toy or object that was at the centre of the dispute. Therese would usually lose out. Her sisters tended to blame her for everything and her mother accepted the sisters' view that Therese was the troublemaker. Therese felt resentful and angry. She knew that she didn't always cause the problem. As a young adult, Therese's relationship with her mother was affected by Therese's belief that her mother didn't support her or believe her. The scars ran deep.

The difficulty in these situations is that if a parent makes a decision and gets it wrong on one occasion, the situation can deteriorate. As a teenager, Therese became so distressed by her relationship with her sisters and her mother that she took to her bed and refused to get out.

Reflect on the battles between brothers and sisters. Children have an investment in blaming a brother or sister for any particular situation that arises. This is a potentially dangerous area. Family harmony can be destroyed. Parents can permanently wreck their relationship with one or more of their children. For whatever reason, it may suit family members to target one person as a problem in order to insulate themselves from having to face more deeply rooted issues.

CASE STUDY: A screaming success?

This family seemed just like most Australian families. Robert ran a successful electrical contracting business and Erica had a part-time nursing position at a major hospital. They had three children. Matilda was a quiet, studious and well-behaved 15-year-old. Tina, on the other hand, was a gregarious and spontaneous 13-year-old who believed that social life was the key to successful living. Last, but far from least, was Jason, a ten-year-old, football-loving early maturer who had every girl in his grade believing that he would be a Hollywood movie star of the future.

Erica complained that the tension between the children had risen to a level that was intolerable. Robert agreed. A typical evening at home would feature Matilda bursting into tears because Jason had gone into her bedroom unannounced and uninvited. She would rush down the stairs, yelling at her mother that she would leave home unless her parents could control Jason's behaviour. Close behind Matilda would be Tina, who would be shrieking about some obscenity that Jason had cast at her. And there was Jason, at the top of the stairs, shouting at all of them that it was lies and protesting his innocence.

Erica, who suffered from migraine headaches, asthma and depression, found that it was too much to cope with. Robert, after his ninth stubbie, would try to calm his wife down and console her with promises that he'd 'give her one tonight'.

What a life! Erica felt that she was going mad, and was on the verge of seeing her family medical practitioner for a referral to a psychiatrist. Yet from her nursing experience, she did not have a great faith in psychiatrists. She believed that they prescribed too many pills, and she couldn't imagine how she would function if she was medicated.

The simplest solution was to 'solve' the problem. Spontaneously, without evaluating the facts, Erica would bellow at Jason to stop what he was doing under threat that she would 'belt him one'. At 95 kg, she was a potential force to be reckoned with. Each night the same scenario would occur. Nothing changed, except the stress levels of all the family members and Jason's resentment of his sisters and mother. Jason became increasingly withdrawn from his family.

Jason, having been identified as the target, was more likely to be accused and punished. The family believed that he was the problem, and the message was reinforced over and over again. Jason felt inwardly hopeless, his marks at school started to decline and he took every opportunity to stay away from home.

Underneath all this chaos was a marriage that was failing. Erica knew that her marriage was in trouble and she felt very vulnerable because of her poor health. Robert had become more reliant on alcohol, to a point where it was affecting his judgement.

We should not underestimate the damage that can be done when we play with our children's reality. If we accuse a child of misbehaving when in reality they haven't, we can do much damage. The accusation of poor behaviour is usually followed by threats and punishments. The downward spiral for that child has begun, and will usually go through a number of phases:

- Initially the child feels anger.
- The anger and feelings of injustice lead to revenge in the form of actual misbehaviour.
- Depression sets in: the child loses interest in family relationships and other things that used to have meaning in their life. They become despondent and disillusioned.
- Mental disturbance comes on, where the child starts to create memories of things that did not actually happen.
- The child comes to believe that he or she was responsible for things that were never done.
- Over a prolonged period of time, the child protects himself or herself by agreeing with those around them. This leads to mental confusion and inward fears of going mad.

Dealing effectively with sibling fights

Fights between children bring with them a highly stressful atmosphere. How quickly irritation, fatigue and despair can set in for the parent. It is essential to remind yourself that you are an adult. You need to choose not to make the children's problem your problem. They have a problem. You don't. Here are some helpful guidelines:

- When disputes occur, avoid sorting out who started it.
- Children can have a vested interest in getting a brother or sister into trouble, so it is unlikely that you would get the truth even if you did investigate.
- Calmly take away the object of the dispute.
- Clearly state to the children that you have no intention of listening to their complaints.
- If necessary, depending on their age, remove children to a second room. When you have decided that they have been there long enough, allow them to come out.

- Give the object back to them with a positive instruction such as 'Take turns, please.'
- Stay calm as an adult. You don't have a problem. The children have to learn to share and cooperate with each other.
- After you have returned the object, do not yell, shout or lecture the children. Keep your message to them very simple: 'Learning to share is important if you want to use this toy or object.'
- Avoiding yelling, shouting or lecturing sends a clear message to the children that the episode is over and is now history. It puts a defined end to the event.

If someone in your family is continually becoming the scapegoat, take it as a clue that there may be underlying problems. Try the guidelines above. Keep repeating them in action. If there is no change in three months, seek professional advice from a psychologist.

Chapter 6
What Is a Normal Teenager?

'Normal' is a troublesome word. Each person is an individual and will mature physically, emotionally, intellectually, socially and spiritually at their own rate. The following list of characteristics is provided as a commonly agreed guide to the more usual behaviours of teenagers. Males and females will share some behaviours, but there will naturally be some differences between the sexes. Many of these differences are biological.

Going Through Stages

The teenage years start with the onset of puberty, and the age at which this occurs can vary significantly between individuals. Psychologists tend to divide the teenage years into three stages – early, middle and late adolescence – in an effort to chart the changes between childhood and adulthood. You would expect to see some common patterns of behaviour in each of these stages.

Early adolescence

As the child reaches puberty, and in the first twelve months thereafter, you may observe:

- increasing vagueness
- talkativeness, but a failure to communicate clearly to adults
- secretiveness and resentment of prying questions from adults
- occasional lying or deceit
- an aggressive attitude to adults
- less attention to cleanliness and hygiene
- wanting to spend more time out of the family home
- height and weight increases
- silliness or giggliness at times
- an emerging interest in the opposite sex.

Middle adolescence

Over the next two years, teenagers may:

- have little concept of cause and effect (hence the need for adults to teach them!)
- believe they are 'superhuman' – that nothing can hurt them
- start to wonder about where they fit into the world
- irritate their parents with the amount of time they spend sleeping
- become more focused on being independent and making their own decisions (Again, adult support in training to do this effectively is important.)

- engage in parent–teenager conflicts (These are normal and necessary, otherwise the teenager will not become independent.)
- confide in each other rather than in adults
- exhibit experimental and risk-taking behaviour, causing parents to age prematurely (This phase is often the time when drinking of alcohol, smoking and other drug-taking or sexual intercourse first occurs.)

Late adolescence

From this point until they reach 20 years of age (although some females would ask if it ever changes for males!), teenagers may:

- enjoy eating with others, and even re-emerge at the family table for dinner
- develop an increasing interest in a relationship with one other person
- need parental respect for opinions that they express, despite the myth that they never take any notice of their parents
- need parents and teachers to respect and accept that they are maturing, in order to grow stronger
- develop a strong interest in what they are going to do with their life, and seem to become more focused
- require sleep in amounts approaching adult levels, and spend less time in bed (at least on their own!)
- drive parents to add on another bathroom, as adults can never get access to the existing one!
- continue to exhibit moodiness but with less regularity.

Iceberg or Volcano?

Adolescents' emotions can be difficult for parents to understand and manage. At the start of adolescence, there are a range of changes to emotional development:

1. The intensity of positive and negative emotions increases
2. Young adolescents experience less positive emotions.
3. There are dramatic changes in mood state.
4. Adolescents become more skilled in using emotions to manage social relationships.
5. Adolescents have more daily fluctuations in self-esteem than adults.

Research in neuro-science suggests that young adolescents experience increased sensitivity to stress and decreased sensitivity to rewards. Adolescents' brains are maturing and it takes some years before the regulatory capacity of the 'thinking' part of the brain becomes effective. In other words, emotions will frequently drive their behaviour.

The young adolescent's increased sensitivity to stress means that both at school and at home they are more likely to be affected by the demands on them. Adults can sometimes be puzzled by their incapacity to handle small challenges, for example:

- a small change in a friendship group
- being organised to take different books and materials to school on different days of the week
- a minor rebuke from a parent.

Adolescents whose families are experiencing problems can suffer frequent and major shifts in mood and emotional state. They don't have the experience or the capacity to 'think' through what is happening like an adult does. They can just be swamped by flooding emotions.

If your family is in crisis, and there is a possibility that the parents will separate, it is very important to understand that adolescents are not mini-adults in the way in which they emotionally respond. Enormous sensitivity to their reactions is going to be needed by both parents.

Teenagers and Study

Encouraging your child to study and do well at school for some reward in the future may lose some of its impact. Parents often interpret this as a 'loss of motivation.' In some cases, the young adolescent may be overwhelmed by the increased demands of schooling. At a time when they are emotionally labile and trying to construct a sense of self-esteem, they may show signs of not being focused on schoolwork. For many adolescents this is a phase that they will work through with empathy, guidance and tolerant management from parents and teaching staff.

A Chemical Cocktail

Research in endocrinology has found that there is clear evidence that moment-to-moment changes in mood states are related to moment-to-moment changes in cortisol levels in adolescents as they go about their daily lives.

Cortisol is a brain-toxic stress hormone that the body naturally produces. It reduces the blood glucose energy supply to the brain. This can cause mental confusion and short-term memory problems. Ever noticed how an adolescent will, even though they are intelligent, have difficulty in thinking through a simple problem? Mental confusion.

Perhaps you have noticed how a young person's short term auditory (or hearing) memory seems to malfunction. No sooner do you ask them to do a couple of things and they have 'forgotten' what you said to them. A lot of this is biologically-driven and is not just the person developing an attitude or behaviour problem. Additionally, cortisol can interfere with the proper function of the brain's neuro-transmitters. These are chemicals that are responsible for sending messages from one brain cell to another.

So beware, as an adult, of drawing false conclusions about a young person's behaviour.

Chronic stress can keep cortisol at an unhealthy levels. Imagine, for a moment, what happens to the young adolescent who is biologically prone to increased sensitivity to stress!

The solution? Physical exercise, a healthy diet, mental stimulation and positive social interaction can all play a part in helping to lower cortisol levels.

As a family, you can provide opportunities and encouragement for your teenager helping them to

- participate in physical exercise of their choice
- eat good nutritious foods
- eat together and converse as part of the family
- attend a school that provides adequate mental stimulation.

A young person who is mentally and physically stimulated has the best opportunity for the brain to physically and mentally grow and mature.

As adults we are aware that emotions drive behaviour. For example, anger triggers off verbal and physical outbursts, while happiness prompts us to smile and to have a more cheerful tone of voice.

Our children will often be volcanoes: explosive, fiery and driven by an inner chemical storm. Parents can often be volcanoes as they struggle to understand their children's behaviour and to control their emotions but they have learnt to moderate their own eruptions.

Volcanic or Iceberg Parents

Parents who are struggling with their own emotional baggage and are burdened by it can become both volcanoes and icebergs.

The iceberg parent is one who emotionally withdraws and becomes very, very cold. They freeze out the people around them. This of course leads to the people around them experiencing increased stress, higher cortisol levels in the blood and all the complications that go with that physiological state.

Adults have learnt to thaw out their iceberg by working on their own emotional baggage and by doing things that encourage a positive emotional state. The beneficiaries are themselves and also their families, colleagues and friends.

My suggestion? Take out the thermometer and do a temperature check on how hot or cold you are!

Teenage Parties

Teenagers are very social beings. It seems that any excuse is good enough to have a party. The word 'party' can cover a multitude of social gatherings. A party may be held for a birthday or simply out of boredom, or a group can decide to get together 'spontaneously'. (This usually means that the last few periods of the school day, particularly on a Friday, have been used to organise the occasion!) As an adult, how do you handle a request from your teenager to go to a party or have one of their own? Take the situation of a request to have a party at your house. Here are some suggested steps:

- Conduct a family conference. This will enable all the family members who are likely to be affected to be involved, and will enable everyone to concentrate on the topic.
- Hear what the teenager has to say about the party.
- Agree on the number of invitees and construct a guest list.
- Determine the venue and hours of the party. Decide first whether you are prepared for your home to be the venue or whether neutral territory like a local hall would be more suitable. Establish and agree on clear starting and finishing times.
- Prepare a written invitation list that will serve on the night as an entry check and to identify gatecrashers.
- Hire a security guard. Ensure that as parents you will be on the property.
- Determine an alcohol policy. This will vary according to the age

of the participants and local laws. BYO beer and light (low-alcohol) drinks, up to a certain quantity, may be a reasonable policy. Mixed drinks, spirits and innocent-looking bottles of cola should be confiscated at the door and securely held until the end of the evening when they can go home with their owners.

- Do not provide or serve alcohol to minors. Have lots of popular non-alcoholic drinks available.

If your child is invited as a guest to a party, on the other hand, consider the following steps:

- Know the name and address of the party.
- Call the adult who is hosting the party and reassure yourself that they will be in attendance. Even if your teenager feels this is to be an unwarranted intrusion, as the adult, still take the responsibility for doing so. If such a procedure is part of the boundaries set when the child is younger, it will not cause discord in the teenage years.
- Make arrangements with your teenager as to a safe way of returning home, before they leave the house, or agree on a pick-up time.
- If your teenager drinks alcohol, encourage reasonable consumption. Set up the expectation that you expect a sober person to return home.
- Advise your teenager to be wary of accepting drinks that have been poured by someone else.

CASE STUDY: Trying it out

Rory's parents were desperate for a holiday but they could not persuade their 16-year-old son that a family holiday would be fun. He insisted on staying at home and convinced his parents that he was old enough to stay in the house on his own. 'Trust me: I'm not a baby,' he told his mother. Feeling they didn't want to treat their son like a child, they agreed to his request.

A couple of days after his parents left, and Rory was organising a party for his friends. Word soon got around and, on the night, dozens of alcohol-laden, excited teenagers descended on the party.

Predictably, except to Rory, the party rapidly got out of control. Neighbours' gardens were trampled, letterboxes were destroyed, the police were called, rapidly followed by TV cameras and the local media.

Rory's parents knew nothing about the party until they turned on the TV the next day at their holiday resort. Imagine their surprise when they realised that the smashed-up police car on the evening news was sitting in front of their own home!

Living with a teenager now means that parents need to have an awareness of how rapidly information can spread via mobile phones and social networking sites on the internet. It is a global community, but it can be fairly threatening when that community arrives on your front doorstep from nowhere expecting to party!

What About More Serious Behaviours?

Do the same techniques apply if a child is engaging in behaviours that are more dangerous than moderate and occasional drinking at parties? If your child is taking an unhealthy amount of drugs, should you just ignore it? If they are engaging in antisocial or criminal behaviour, do you simply turn a blind eye? Ask yourself: 'What is an appropriate adult response?' In your attempt to wrestle with this question, take off your parent hat and put on your adult hat.

As a society and as adults, we cannot condone antisocial or illicit drug-taking behaviour. Breaking the law is not an option for responsible adults. A society can only be cohesive and stable if its members agree to and abide by the rules. Turning a blind eye to potentially dangerous and illegal behaviour is not an adult response.

Assess the situation you face. Do so honestly and do not get caught up with assumptions. Finding a bong in your child's room doesn't mean that they are addicted to marijuana or that heroin is being used.

CASE STUDY: Trying it out

Julian was 15 when his friends suggested he try marijuana. His parents were unaware of his experimentation until one day when his mother Dawn was giving his bedroom an annual vacuum clean. There, underneath young Julian's bed, was a bamboo contraption that her husband identified as a bong. Dawn was devastated.

The adult response from Dawn and her husband would be to be alert to the emergence of Julian's interest in marijuana. Vigilance would be the next step. Are there signs of negative change in Julian's behaviour that warrant intervention?

Problem behaviour differs from normal adolescent behaviour. Determine, in your mind, the differences between the two. Experimenting is a part of the growth process. Children will experiment with clothes, hairstyle and friendships, and they may try different sports and hobbies. They might also experiment with some of the 'forbidden' aspects of life including sex, alcohol, cigarettes and illicit drugs. Rock and roll or dance music, however, will often continue to be a permanent feature of life continuing into old age! Once tasted, many forbidden fruits are abandoned. Think of the number of adults you have heard retelling a tale of smoking a cigarette as a child and vowing and declaring that they would never smoke again.

Problem behaviour is often behaviour that has a high risk or potential for self-destruction which continues through the 'occasional use' phase and is adopted as a more permanent feature of a person's lifestyle. This is the kind of behaviour that may need closer scrutiny.

Adolescence is the time when some of the serious mental illnesses of adult life first appear. Although they are not all that common, illnesses including schizophrenia, depression and personality disorders can emerge. As an adult, use your powers of observation to gather information that will help you decide whether professional help is desirable.

Depression, in particular, has been estimated to affect about 20 per cent of adolescents. Symptoms to be aware of are:
- lengthy periods of unexplained fatigue
- sustained changes to appetite or eating patterns
- difficulty in sleeping or continuing disturbances to sleep patterns
- loss of interest in school
- marks at school falling off
- lack of interest in things that you would normally expect to be of interest
- periods of self-imposed isolation
- loss of interest in developing or pursuing friendships
- looking sad and gloomy frequently
- indulging in self-destructive behaviour.

If a combination of these symptoms also coincides with more regular illicit drug or alcohol use, it would be wise to seek professional advice. The connection between depression and suicide, or an attempt at suicide, is well documented.

The other cluster of behaviours that signal a potential problem are the high-risk behaviours. Some examples of these are:
- over-confident use of alcohol or drugs
- irresponsible sexual behaviour
- recklessness in a motor vehicle
- illegal use of a motor vehicle
- daredevil exploits

- contempt for personal safety and that of others
- seeking friends' approval through dangerous behaviour.

Teenagers, in general, have a very low ability to visualise their own vulnerability. They are usually healthy and strong and have good reflexes. This can expose them to higher risks, as their sense of caution is lower than that of adults. As mentioned above, adolescents have a limited capacity to link cause and effect in advance of their actions. This is why it is important, when they make an error of judgement, that they are given the opportunity to quietly and clearly learn from their experience.

If, in your view, a teenager is engaging in more than one high-risk behaviour, seek a professional opinion. If high-risk behaviour also occurs with any of the symptoms of underlying depression mentioned above, seek advice. Again, be aware that any of these behaviours that are occurring while the young person has a poor relationship with their parents is a reason to seek professional advice. Speak to your medical practitioner or a psychologist.

As adults, we don't have to be experts on everything. Look, observe and talk to a professional if you are concerned by what you see, or if you feel confused about what is happening within your family. It's better to check with someone who is independent than harbour constant fear or doubt. Seek factual information about the issue that concerns you.

Knowing your child and observation are the keys. Don't rely on questioning your child. It is not uncommon for young people to be unable or unwilling to express what is happening to them. They can often feel things happening but are unable to clearly identify or talk about their feelings. Professionals can sometimes be helpful here to enable the young person to express themselves.

CASE STUDY: No smoke without fire

Lyle was just about to celebrate his seventeenth birthday. Until he was 14, he was described by his parents as a 'pretty normal kid'. He had settled into secondary school but in Year 8 he seemed to lose interest in schoolwork and his grades started to slip. His parents thought it was normal teenage behaviour and, in itself, not all that significant. Over the next 12 months, there was little improvement in his schoolwork. This was the year that Lyle admitted to his parents that he 'smoked a bit of dope'. He was very vague about the amount he was smoking or the frequency with which he smoked. His friendship circle changed. His parents saw less of his swimming team friends, who had previously always seemed to live at their house. The new friends seemed less interested in sport, more sloppy in their appearance and less communicative with them as parents. They were, according to his mother's description, 'typical dope-smoking surfie dropouts'. Lyle spent more time in his bedroom and less time with the family.

It was in the August of Lyle's Year 9 that his mother noticed he was showering less frequently. He also seemed to be overly fussy about what he would eat and not eat. He would raid the fridge late at night, but seem to have little appetite at normal meal times. His facial expressions seemed to change and according to his father he had a 'trance-like' appearance. It was at this stage that his parents started to think about seeking outside help. Lyle's final school report and a troubling parent–teacher meeting at the end of the year confirmed for his parents that all was not well. Over the Christmas holidays, Lyle and one of his new friends went surfing in a highly dangerous area.

At the start of Year 10, Lyle presented as a tall, athletic young man who looked as though he needed a good feed and a good night's sleep. He had been partying for weeks and playing life a bit hard.

Initially, Lyle seemed reluctant to talk about himself and his lifestyle. When he did start to communicate, it became clearer that he was confused about what was happening to him. He had fallen in love with a girl in Year 9 that he didn't think his parents would approve of, and had kept hidden from them his relationship with her. This had caused stress, as he had previously been fairly open with his parents about what he did. The girl had initiated a sexual relationship and he had lost his virginity to her. She was very critical of his sexual performance and had labelled him 'gay' before she broke the relationship off, something that he hadn't shared with either parent. When directly questioned about suicidal thoughts, Lyle admitted that he had been thinking increasingly frequently about it.

Once Lyle was able to express his fears, doubts and despair, he was able to put his life into perspective. All was not hopeless and he was able to distinguish between real concerns and worries that had no substance. He is now doing Year 11, has a new circle of friends, is more balanced in his lifestyle and is enjoying a new relationship with a girl that he met through a friend at a party.

Keeping the Door Open

The most frustrating thing that parents experience with children who engage in more dangerous behaviours is a sense of profound despair and powerlessness. The maxim that the only person you can change is yourself, despite being a reality, provides little comfort to the parent who is witnessing their child quietly destroying themselves.

If you are in the situation of watching a child continue on a downward spiral, consider some adult actions that you can take:

- Observe and record the behaviour. Jotting down key episodes and dates will enable a more accurate record to be compiled. This will avoid difficulties with recall at a later stage. This record, at an appropriate time, may be very useful for the treating professional.

- Monitor the safety aspects of the child's behaviour. Is there a likelihood of an accident or fire? Is there a firearm in the home that is accessible to the child? Are there steps that need to be taken to keep the family safe?
- Do these things confidentially, without other children in the family knowing. It is not a policing action. It is an attempt to objectively note what is occurring.
- Do some homework on available treatment options – find out what is available, what it costs, and how readily you can gain access to the service you might need.
- Talk with your family medical practitioner, or other appropriate professional, about what is occurring. This may lead to ideas being shared and give you access to information and support systems that are currently unknown to you.
- Talk with your partner, if you have one, or a close friend or relative.
- Avoid repetitious lectures to the child who is experiencing difficulties. This will minimise the risk of their becoming resentful and angry. The goal is for the child to feel comfortable in asking for support from you when they are ready to change.
- Clearly set the goal of keeping communication open with the family member who is in trouble. Communication is the prelude to healing.
- Monitor your language. Listen to what you say and how you say it. Rehearse before you open your mouth. Some ideas are outlined below.
- Have an emergency strategy mapped out in your mind. Do you call the police? Is the local emergency department at the hospital accessible? Are phone numbers readily to hand?

Communication Is the Key
Language is a powerful tool for us to use:

Keeping communication open with the troubled child is the goal.

When the teenager's behaviour is unacceptable and is causing distress to other family members, emotions will be running high. It can be very easy to give voice to these emotions. Stay focused on the goal, which is keeping communication with the child open, so that when the they want help, there is a better chance of them coming to you for that help.

Watching a child engage in self-destructive behaviour can be heartbreaking for any parent. Difficult as it will be, repeatedly bring back to your conscious mind that picture of your child as a successful adult. No matter how unrealistic it might seem, never let that picture fade.

This will be the biggest test of your capacity as an adult to focus on your own behaviour as a means of enabling the troubled young person to develop an awareness of what they are doing to themselves and others.

Keeping Negative Emotions Under Control
Remember this:

The moment you raise your voice and shout is when you lose and the child wins.

It is as simple as that – 100 per cent guaranteed – no matter how important the issue. Once you lose your cool and become emotionally entangled in an issue, you send a very clear message to the child that you are vulnerable, and the child has enormous power to upset you. For children, it can be entertaining to see how they can change the mood of a parent. It can be an adrenalin rush for the child who, excited and amused by the spectacle of you making a fool of yourself, will be seeking to revisit the experience.

If you have raised your voice, started to shout, or feel your emotions boiling up, choose to walk away, no matter how right or wrong you might be. The reason: you are going to lose and the child is going to win. Guaranteed!

Children watch and observe their parents very closely. They'll soon detect if they have emotionally wounded you and you are losing control of yourself. Often you will hear parents say that they know their children very well. Sometimes we forget that our children also know us very well and have picked out our weaknesses.

A pre-teen child might comply with the authoritarian demand you have shouted at them, but as they do so they will plot their revenge. Instead of learning to deal with life, the child now focuses their mind on the unhealthy emotion of revenge. Time spent engaging in these thoughts is likely to result in the development of unhealthy emotional responses to life. Yes, in the short-term a child might comply through fear. However, the seed has been sown for an unhealthy emotional response to become established. In addition, the child is now locked into a power battle with you. The war may not yet have started, but it won't be too far away. Power battles destroy enjoyment of the family and a true sense of what family means.

Pull out. Go and hide in your special place, the bedroom, kitchen, garden or toilet and calm down. You'll be much more successful when you have given yourself space to regain your composure and put on your adult hat. The toilet is a great place to have space to think. Retreating to your bedroom may result in the child following you. Another good strategy, shared with me by a client, is to go to your Tupperware cupboard and tidy it up!

As an adult you can still be human. You don't have to be an expression-less robot. The very occasional lapse into an emotional outburst will serve to remind the child that you too have feelings and that just occasionally you reach the end of your tether.

Recognise the Child's Expression of Feelings

Not uncommonly, parents become emotional and shout at their children when the children express their feelings. It can be a very threatening experience to have a child unleash their negative emotions upon you. However, this situation is not a threat to your parental authority. It is the child discovering their emotional world and trying to give expression to it.

We all occasionally feel uncomfortable or troubled and find it difficult to express this accurately in words. It is even more difficult for children to appropriately express their feelings. The brain is maturing and their language skills might not meet the challenge. An inability to clearly identify and express feelings can lead to anger and outbursts of foul language. This is a symptom of the child struggling to articulate their emotions. An adult who witnesses this outburst, or who is the recipient of unpleasant language, can become of-fended and distressed. Stand back from the experience and be aware that, as an adult, you don't have a problem. The child has a difficulty in identifying their feelings and giving appropriate expression to them.

Reflect for a moment on the importance of learning to identify a feeling and being able to express it. Learning to put feelings into words enables the brain to organise and make sense of the experience. Emotional self-awareness emerges. Awareness of feelings is essential to effective living. In order to achieve this goal, a child needs to be listened to and coached to identify and express feelings. This takes time – there are no shortcuts. Parents tend to focus on cutting through the emotion to quickly resolve an issue. This rarely works or helps the child to develop.

Helping a child through the process enables them to change their own mood state. They learn to take responsibility for changing themselves, rather than blame others for how they feel. This is a stepping stone in emotional growth.

CASE STUDY: The pressure will blow

Kai had come to Australia with his parents three years earlier. He spoke little English and entered an English Language Centre prior to going to school. It was a big transition for him, to a new country, with a new language, different culture and different expectations from teachers, and it left him with a sense of being very isolated. He was tired from the day-to-day effort of adjusting to everything new in his life, including the high-rise flat that his family lived in, which lacked the open space of the rural area in China in which he had lived. One day he came home from school and unleashed his feelings on his parents. There was very little logic in what he said. It was an outburst of abuse directed at his family for bringing him to Australia. He was angry and hurt.

Kai's parents were shocked by the change in their son. His behaviour transgressed all boundaries of decency and respect. The parents were in a state of shock and felt their whole world collapsing around them.

It took some time for Kai's parents to outgrow their parental shock and hurt. They maintained, for some weeks, that it was their right to be offended. This was fine, but they had to live with the consequence: sadness, despair, anger and resentment. All of which are good for the health!

For some people, anger can be exhilarating and energising. Children who constantly resort to angry mood states are at risk of relying on anger to give them a lift. This is a potentially dangerous outcome of not learning to deal with anger. There are more positive ways to feel exhilarated.

Research indicates that aerobic exercise is an effective way of changing mood state. In particular, if a person is mildly depressed or in a bad mood state, exercise can help them to change the mood to a more positive one. Your mum was right when she said 'Go for a walk, it'll do you good.' Suggest that the child go for a walk, run or cycle. If it is appropriate, you might even offer to go with them. Help the child to see that there is nothing wrong in feeling a particular emotion, it is the way that it is expressed that is important.

As adults, there is a responsibility on us to teach our children to use exercise as a means to positively change their mood and to feel more in control of themselves. It's better than popping pills! The power of personal example is the key.

Children who are depressed, anxious or angry don't learn or do well at schoolwork. The most likely reason is that, no matter how strong their intelligence, negative emotions will overwhelm their concentration and they will not be able to absorb new information or think sequentially. As an example, think about the subject of mathematics. It requires the following skills:

- An ability to use prior learning. Each thing learned is the foundation for the next new piece of learning. A lack of understanding in one area leads to an inability to learn the next piece of knowledge.
- An ability to follow through a process step by step. This is what psychologists and teachers refer to as sequential thought. To achieve sequential thought, the mind needs to be clear and focused on the process at hand. If the mind is deflected or absorbed by inner worries or feelings of despondency or anger, this process cannot occur. Hence very bright but troubled children can have their mathematics grades deteriorate.

Remind Yourself That You Are the Adult

Choose not to be thrown off your inner balance by the taunts and barbs of your offspring. In times of provocation and challenge, take a second to state silently to yourself 'I am the adult'. It is important to do this consciously and deliberately. You'll soon forget otherwise.

Be confident in yourself and your approach. You'll soon know when you have lost confidence in your adult status: you become like a child, raising your voice, yelling and being driven by emotion. I remember seeing a very successful businessman reduced to a screaming lunatic by his child. You have to see this kind of thing to believe it. How could someone of above-average intelligence, with a track record in commerce and sophisticated staff management skills, be driven to the point of screaming and yelling and total confusion about his child? Easily! – he kept seeing himself as a parent. He played all the traditional parent power games and forgot that he was an adult. Like many of us, he had slipped into the role of 'father' without giving it much thought.

If clear thinking has given way to emotionally based ramblings and ravings, with threats of diabolical and long-lasting punishments that you are going to inflict upon the child, it is time to recognise that you've lost the plot. We all make mistakes at times. There is no prescription that says we have to be perfect. Learn from your mistake and regain your composure. Remember the saying:

Successful people fail, but they fail less often.

Choose to change yourself.

Have you noticed that often, as a child becomes louder and noisier, the parent follows suit, increasing the volume of their voice and becoming more emotional in their tone. Who is leading whom? Why would you choose, as a sane and sensible adult, to give your child the power to drive you to insanity?

If you recognise that in the past you have chosen to allow your child to manipulate your mood, tone of voice and expression, just as a puppeteer manipulates a puppet, you can choose to respond in a different way.

Nobody is perfect. But we can all choose to see how we are behaving and to make adjustments to how we act.

So, you want a better deal as a parent, more harmony in the home, less stress from behaviour problems? Then choose to make it happen. Start working on yourself.

Hyperactive Kids

Recall our example of Mark in the case study *Keeping to your game plan* on page 92. Children who suffer from diagnosed conditions such as attention deficit disorder are among the most challenging ones to live with. They are so loud, noisy, unsettled and intrusive that they can invade your private space and cripple the ways in which a family interacts. So often the parents' attention is directed towards changing the child, with little effect. The child leads and everyone becomes louder and noisier in a fight for attention. What happens to you as the adult, living with this child?

One of the simplest ways to improve this situation is to teach the parents to focus on their behaviour. Assisting the parent to see that they are fatigued, emotionally exhausted and louder in *their* behaviour as a result of what the child is doing is the first step. Teaching the parents to become quieter and softer in their tone of voice, in response to the yelling and ranting of the child, immediately improves the situation and enables more control.

When the parents are reminded that they are the adults and they can withdraw their attention from the child during periods of wild behaviour, the child is left with little choice but to adjust to the new conditions. Normally, the child is in such disbelief at the renewed self-control of their parents that initially the behaviour becomes worse. This is an effort by the child to test out the parents. Quiet and committed resolve on the part of the parents will result in the child burning out the emotion, and some level of stable behaviour will be achieved. (This also works effectively in combination with other forms of treatment for the child).

This technique not only works with extreme forms of behaviour but with more common behaviours as well. The key to achieving change is to stop focusing on the child's behaviour and to stop trying to change it. Focus on your own behaviour, modify it and then just keep repeating your new behaviour and watch what happens. Don't expect an instant cure. Fake it till you make it! The child will temporarily become worse. Just be confident, as an adult, that your technique is well thought out. There is a logic in your approach. You are avoiding negative emotional expressions. You are doing no harm. Hang in there. Don't give up.

Often parents will achieve success in making such changes but then abandon their approach, revert back to the parent hat and all the old parenting behaviours, and wonder why things deteriorate. Old habits die hard. Just believe in yourself as an adult. You have thought through your strategy. Keep focusing on how you are responding to situations that occur. Don't let your child call the tune.

Do not waver. Do not bend. You are not a tree.

Teaching Values and Beliefs

Being an adult also means that you have developed a set of values and beliefs. You might for example believe:

- that success comes from hard work
- that education is very important
- that honesty and integrity are essential in our lives
- that taking personal responsibility for your actions is a key to living.

And there will be many more. These values and beliefs can be taught to your child, not by incessant talking, as I have suggested before, but by the power of personal example.

Your children will observe how you live and they will make their judgement on what you stand for. This is why it is important that you, as an adult, model what you desire for your child. Look at the four values above. These can be demonstrated in your daily life. If, for example, you believe education is very important, demonstrate this through such things as:

- your own willingness to read and learn
- becoming involved, in some way, in your child's school.

The 'Do as I say, not as I do' routine is fatal, as well as immature. This is the 45-year-old going on 15! Our children may partly or wholly accept what we believe in. They may add or subtract from our value system. Society progresses by challenging ideas and beliefs from one generation to the next. It is our duty to train the next generation to be intelligent in their questioning of the ways in which things have been done by their parents.

Once upon a time, and not so long ago, our forebears believed that war was honourable and that to die for king and country was appropriate. They also believed that a male was the head of the household and that women shouldn't vote or receive equal pay for equal work. They brought their children up with those values. What would have happened if those values had been left unchallenged by a compliant generation in the 1960s and 1970s?

Society does change. For centuries, funerals in most European cultures have been solemn affairs. They were religious occasions and were scripted to reinforce prevailing beliefs about life, death, sin, hell, heaven and salvation. Life and death were antonyms. As I write, we are on the verge of significant change. New Age thinking has created the concept that death is just another stage of life. Funerals aren't automatically held in churches or chapels anymore. The bereaved participate more actively in the design and implementation of the service. The solemn tones of a funeral service are now replaced by joyous, often laughter-filled celebrations of an individual's life. People now expect the truth about the deceased's life. More people choose to write their own eulogy rather than risk the fantasy constructed by someone else. Church music is replaced by a favourite CD.

Yet we are so easily threatened by the next generation's challenges to our views and authority. We enjoy being in our comfort zone. Perhaps we are fearful that our children might have an insight that we don't possess!

The Youth of Today
Does have respect and morals
Like we did in our day
But we, the Youth of Yesterday
Have changed the environment
And have imposed our ideals on them.
We are no different from our peers

And the Youth of Today
Are no different from us.
They have just got to live
With the legacy of the world
Which the Youth of Yesterday, which is us,
Have left them.

—Mick Whatham, 'Days of Yore', in *Days of Yore*

However you choose to bring up your children, you can maintain your values and beliefs – you don't have to compromise them. You can help your child to understand why you hold them. Teach them. Demonstrate them in your daily life. But also be prepared to learn.

So often, parents make all their decisions based exclusively on their own view of the world, their previous experience or their own fears. This is noticeable, for example, in situations where the parent:

- has been less than perfect themslves as a child and wishes to prevent their child from having a behaviour problem (perhaps this is fear of genetic transmission?)
- has experienced some form of trauma in a similar situation
- has absorbed too much advice from well-meaning relatives or friends
- is concerned by other adults' reactions to them as parents as a result of the decision. *Parents* are susceptible to peer pressure. *Adults* aren't susceptible. They trust their own judgement.

Be open to your child's point of view. Avoid the excuse that the child is immature and that their opinion is therefore not worth listening to. Of course the child will often be immature and unsophisticated in their view. They are not yet adults. Hear what they want. Do not be afraid to listen to your child: they might surprise you. Listen to what is important for them and take this into account in negotiating or talking through how a situation is to be handled.

The supplementary benefit of this technique is that children are learning another important skill through the process. They are experiencing at first hand the importance of being listened to. They will, in turn, be inclined to listen to other people as they move through life, and to acknowledge their views and feelings.

So often, one hears wives complain of chauvinistic husbands who don't listen to what they want or how they feel. As children, these chauvinistic husbands were trained by a parent or parents not to have their feelings acknowledged. They never learned the skill, and in adult life they pay the price in their relationships.

Chauvinists are also trained by mothers who are willing to be slaves to their families. For their own emotional needs, these mothers enjoy pandering to their sons and having them dependent on them.

When you are being open to your child's views, do so with genuine intent. Don't mutter under your breath that this is something that you have to do to get it out of the way so that you can then achieve what you want. Children are very skilled in measuring sincerity.

CASE STUDY: I was like that once, man

Kelvin wanted to go to a rock festival that was being held in the country over the Easter vacation. He was up to date with all his homework and felt he deserved a break. He knew that his father, in his youth, had been a hippie, and amusedly recalled the photos of his father with long hair, naked, standing in a stream at the Yarra Falls Love-in. It seemed so hard to imagine that it really was his father, who now, as one of Melbourne's leading gynaecologists, drove a BMW to and from work and purchased his suits in Rome each year.

It was breakfast time. Father had enjoyed a good sleep and Kelvin seized the moment. Over a bowl of muesli, Kelvin shared his vision of a perfect Easter. Father smiled. He was immediately thrown back to his own youth and memories of naked, nubile flesh, mud, sweet aromas of takeaway food and the cleansing taste of a cold tinnie. The parent voice leapt into his mind: 'Would Kelvin be safe and sensible?' Choosing not to directly respond to the voice, he put on his adult hat and asked Kelvin about the arrangements he had made for transport, accommodation, food and cost. They amicably discussed them in detail.

You might even compromise if it is not an important issue. Displaying some flexibility on non-major items is a sign of adult maturity. We expect this in the workplace. As adults we accommodate others' needs and flex to meet them. In return, other adults will accommodate our needs when the opportunity arises. Why shouldn't your child expect the same to occur at home?

Stay calm and firm, even though your child might throw a tantrum in response. You are the adult. Would you choose to be hooked in by a childish tantrum? Not only are you stating your personal beliefs and values, but you are once again setting boundaries that are firm and consistent. Nothing creates more insecurity than inconsistency. The teenager may kick against the boundary but at least they have found the limits. They will know and understand your position. Somewhere, sometime, someone has to stand for something. If the boundary fences keep moving, the child learns that there is little security in life and little point in believing in anything because it all keeps changing to meet a new situation. Stand firm. Stand as a true adult.

Do not waver. Do not bend. You are not a tree.

I am amazed at the number of parents who cave in under these circumstances, resulting in them having no idea where their child is at any particular hour of the day or night. Why do parents abandon what they believe to be right and true?

The answer is simple: out of fear. Fear that their child will not like them, that they won't be friends. Fear that their child won't love them. Fear that they are different to other parents and might be seen in an unfavourable light by those parents. Fear that, if they were to give expression to their values and set boundaries, the child might rebel even more and they would lose total control. Better to give in and be flexible and maybe the child will conform in some other areas. They fear that setting boundaries will alienate the child!

Ask yourself, 'How absurd is this?' Just ensure that the child grows up with boundaries. If you are motivated by fear – you've lost the plot. You have chosen to let inappropriate negative emotions drive your life. Negative emotions have negative outcomes. You will pay the price.

Believe in yourself and the values that you hold dear. If your child, in the short term, decides that they don't like you, they have the problem – you don't. Get on with your life with an air of calm confidence. Demonstrate to your child that you are secure as a person. This will force the child to reassess their view of you.

Fake it till you make it!

Just ensure that you are not being unnecessarily rigid or dogmatic. Don't ram your core values down your child's throat. Brainwashing your child gives little recognition to their capacity to think and to make judgements. Quietly explain to the child why those values are important to you. Teach them by example that you can balance flexibility and values. Tolerance is a key skill to develop. In order to be a successful adult, your child will need to demonstrate tolerance to others in their adult life.

Chapter **7**
Working As a Team

Adults communicate with each other. If you are bringing up a child with a partner, take the opportunity to discuss issues together. Plan ahead. Work out the boundaries that are agreed between you. Get your act together before you go onstage with your child. This is a proven principle for actors and it can work for you.

Entering in to a conversation, with a child, lacking a common approach between parents will result in division and anxiety.

CASE STUDY: The big sleepover

Mary had turned 17 and felt that she should be able to have her boyfriend sleep over. Making love in the back of his secondhand Daihatsu was very uncomfortable and unpleasant. Luke was a big boy. Each time they made love, she dreamt of her warm and comfortable double bed at home that her parents had so generously bought her for her sixteenth birthday. Her parents liked Luke. He was intelligent, a good student and sportsman. The moment had come to discuss her needs with her parents.

Mary's father turned white. Mary's mother smiled. She was satisfied that her suspicion that Mary was having sex had been confirmed. Father said that it would have never been permitted in his day and it certainly wasn't going to occur under his roof. Mother told Father to be more accommodating and to get himself out of the dark ages. Father became angry and poured himself a beer. For the next hour Mother and Father debated the morality of premarital sex, parental responsibility, values, standards, pregnancies, child adoption and abortion. Mary sobbed. Mother yelled and Father became more insistent that he was right. Finally, Father said he was going out. Mother took two of her favourite painkillers and Mary yelled at them both for being so lacking in understanding, burst into tears again, retreated into her bedroom, slammed the door and dialled up Luke on her mobile phone.

Nothing had been resolved or agreed. Each family member became more anxious and unsettled. What would have been a more adult approach? Adults control their environment. It might have been wiser for Mary's parents to use the parliamentary technique of 'putting the question on notice', thereby allowing themselves time to consider the issue and to give a thoughtful response. This would have given them space and privacy to talk through the issues before both sitting down with Mary and discussing her request.

Lack of agreement between the parents was likely to have been a major contributor to the mess that they ended up in. Inconsistency, as I stated previously, can be a major contributor to instability and insecurity. Nobody feels secure when there is an atmosphere of disagreement. Inconsistency can occur where one parent is 'hard' and the other 'soft'. Some parents have suggested to me that this creates a balance in the style of parenting for the children. Rubbish! What it creates is a mixed and confused message to the children about what is acceptable and unacceptable behaviour.

The differences that exist between parents can lead to arguments and fights. As the situation becomes more emotional, there is a higher risk of inappropriate and insensitive remarks being exchanged between parents. More distress is caused. Children who witness their parents arguing with each other, particularly over some issue involving the children, see a wonderful opportunity to manipulate and exploit the situation to their advantage.

CASE STUDY: Divide and rule #1

Adam was 16 years of age. He had been invited to a friend's sixteenth birthday party and he was very keen to go. Adam's father, Terry, told him that he could go if he washed the family car before he went. When it was time to go to the party and the car remained unwashed, Terry said 'You can't go to the party yet. You've been messing around all day. Get out and wash the car.'

At this, Adam's mother, Muriel, rushed in and said 'You can't say that to Adam. He has been looking forward to this party for ages and it will embarrass him in front of his friends if he is late.'

Adam agreed and angrily yelled at his father 'You are so unfair!'

Terry told Muriel that she was weak and Adam that he was 'a lazy little good-for-nothing bludger.'

Muriel cuddled Adam and then burst into tears. She grabbed the car keys and drove Adam to the party.

So what did Adam learn? That being irresponsible is alright. Mum said so! The message was clear: ignore what Dad says. The next time Dad tries to implement a consequence for Adam's actions, it is not going to happen. Adam can effectively do what he likes. Mum will be there to rescue him.

Remember the old maxim:

United you stand and divided you fall!

Unstable conditions lead to anarchy. We see this in countries that have been politically destabilised. People run riot. Similar things can occur in our homes!

So what can parents do? The following ideas may help:

- Try to agree – in advance – on what the basic behaviours and responsibilities should be.
- Agree – again, ahead of time – on what the consequences or outcomes should be.
- If one parent disagrees with another, do not do so in front of the children. Take it to another room if necessary.
- If the child comes running to one parent, complaining about the other parent's decision, do not buy into it. Simply say 'Dad (Mum) must have a good reason for saying that. Go and talk to him (her).'
- If an error was made by a parent, then either let the decision stand and agree as parents to handle it differently next time, or change the decision, if the parents have privately agreed to do so. Ensure that it is the parent who originally made the agreement with the child, who brings the changed decision to the child's attention. This will maintain an atmosphere of cooperation between the parents. It is important that the child sees this occur.

Let's re-examine Adam's situation.

CASE STUDY: Divide and rule #2

Adam was 16 years of age. He had been invited to a friend's sixteenth birthday party and he was very keen to go. Adam's father, Terry, told him that he could go if he washed the family car before he went. When it was time to go to the party and the car remained unwashed, Terry said 'You can't go to the party yet. You've been messing around all day. Get out and wash the car.'

Adam said that he had forgotten to do it and promised faithfully that it would be done by lunchtime tomorrow. Terry was unimpressed and reminded Adam that growing up and having more freedom meant that he had to take some responsibilities. Adam's mother, Muriel, was observing the conversation between father and son.

Adam appealed to his mother. 'What do you reckon, Mum? I don't think that's fair.'

'Don't ask me. You have an agreement with your father. Sort it out with him,' she advised.

This was not the answer Adam wanted. He stormed off to his bedroom to ring a mate and engage in a bit of verbal parent-bashing.

When Adam was out of the room, Terry and Muriel discussed the situation and agreed that he was fairly conscientious and usually did the right thing, but as a typically

.dreamy adolescent, on this occasion he had become sidetracked. They agreed privately that if the car was washed by lunchtime tomorrow they would be happy.

Adam returned to the room, pleading with his parents to understand how important this party was to him. Terry said 'Adam, you have failed in your responsibility. You need to learn. If you have the car washed by lunchtime tomorrow that will be fine. But be very clear in your mind that if you fail to do so, your mother and I are agreed that you will loose your privilege to go out for the next four weekends. So listen up. Think about it. Be very sure in your mind, right here and now, about what will happen.'

'Thanks,' said Adam.

'That's fine. But you tell me what you understand our agreement to be.'

Adam repeated the agreement.

'You are okay about that?' asked Terry.

'Fine,' said Adam as he rushed off to the bathroom to gel his hair for the fourth time in the last hour.

There is a difference between the two management styles. This difference resulted in two opposing outcomes. In the first example, Adam's parents clearly had their parent hats on. Notice the sequence of events:

- Adam and his father had a clear agreement. The car would be washed by Adam before he went to the party.
- Adam failed to wash the car.
- Terry responded to Adam's failure by restating the agreement.

So far, everything is on track, but it now disintegrates into a mess:

- Adam's mother interferes and criticises his father's decision in front of her son.
- Adam takes advantage of the difference in his parents' views and criticises his father.
- Terry responds angrily and criticises both his wife and son.
- The situation becomes emotional.
- Muriel rushes to Adam's aid.
- Muriel counteracts Terry's decision by driving Adam to the party.

In the second example, the parents had their adult hats firmly on:

- Adam and his father had a clear agreement. The car would be washed by Adam before he went to the party.
- Adam failed to wash the car.
- Terry responded to Adam's failure by restating the agreement.
- Adam wanted to renegotiate the agreement.
- Adam attempted to draw his mother into the conversation.
- Muriel declined to be involved.

- The parents discussed the situation in Adam's absence.
- Terry, with whom Adam had the original agreement, renegotiated with Adam.
- Terry sought Adam's clear understanding of the new agreement.
- Adam was required to state his understanding and consent to the changed agreement.

In fact, Adam went to the party and did wash the car the next day before lunchtime. He had learnt a good lesson about responsibility, fairness and flexibility.

How Flexible Can You Be?

We are all human. No matter how conscientious and efficient we are, there will be times when we do not act with an appropriate level of efficiency. Some days we might be tired or off-color. At other times we will simply not be in the mood to do what we should be doing. Can we, as parents, be flexible without causing a problem by sending mixed messages to our children?

Be relieved – the answer is yes. As parents we are trying to prepare our children for the outside world. We want them to be responsible, achieving and gaining satisfaction in the various areas of their lives. But the world is not a perfect place. Flexibility is needed to accommodate the humanness of others.

Yes, we can be flexible. We can acknowledge that people are not always totally responsible or efficient. How we communicate this flexibility to our children is the factor that we need to be focused on.

Re-examine the second example above. Adam did not wash the car, yet he was able to go to the party. The manner in which this came about is the clue as to how to be flexible. Adam still learned a valuable lesson.

Forgiveness for Errors

You and your children will make mistakes. To be a good parent, you do not have to be perfect. If you have made a mistake, act like an adult and apologise to your child. Learning to admit to others that we are sometimes wrong is a very important skill in living. Teach your child, by your own example, that saying sorry is a virtue.

CASE STUDY: Who's that standing in my house?

Hugh was very tired. He drove into the garage at home at 8 pm after a 14-hour day. He had caught a 6 am flight to Melbourne for a business meeting and returned to Sydney on the 6 pm flight. The day had not gone well. The business deal was collapsing and Hugh was feeling anxious about the consequences of possibly losing the deal.

As Hugh walked into the house, he found a strange male person at the foot of the stairs. He was immediately angry. 'Why does my daughter invite her friends over on a week night?'

'I see you've decided to go home now,' Hugh said to the young man sarcastically.

The young man was so startled by this greeting that he muttered something and walked out of the front door. He could take a hint.

Hugh proceeded to the bedroom to change his clothes. Shortly afterwards, his daughter appeared in the bedroom enquiring about the whereabouts of her friend. Hugh told her that the young man had chosen to go home. His daughter was furious and grilled her father as to why this had occurred. The truth emerged and she was most upset. She demanded an apology and insisted that her father drive with her down the road to the public telephone box where her friend was most likely to be calling his mother to pick him up. Grudgingly, Hugh agreed. A brief and curt apology was offered to the young man by Hugh and they all drove back to the house.

Even though Hugh was reluctant to apologise, his daughter commented some days later that she had appreciated this action. The young man and the daughter continue to be friends and now, upon visiting, he is treated by Hugh with a higher level of courtesy.

Revisit Your Definition Of Love

Parents love their children. Many of the actions that parents take in relation to their children are described as occurring because they love them. Love can be blind. Examine closely your own definition of love for your child and how you might use it to justify your actions. Consider the example of Maria and her daughter Houla.

CASE STUDY: It's an ill wind

Maria loved her daughter, Houla, who had just celebrated her eleventh birthday. Houla had a most unfortunate flatulence problem that caused discomfort for her immediate family and embarrassment during larger family events and social moments. As she grew up, Houla received so much attention for her flatulence that she soon learned that a good way to redirect parental attention away from her two younger brothers was to engulf the room in the most unpleasant odour. Visits to the family doctor and purchases of aerosol room deodorisers did little to improve the family's comfort. Maria even changed the family diet in a desperate attempt to ease the problem. After lengthy discussions with Houla about favourite and acceptable foods, the whole family found they were losing weight but the core problem continued. Maria's mother was consulted, aunts were brought into the discussion and Houla's father Tony threatened to leave home if things did not improve. Houla continued to be a very happy child. Maria, to her embarrassment, raised Houla's problem with her class teacher, in fear that Houla might be losing friendships because of her unfortunate condition. To her surprise, the class teacher reported that Houla did not suffer from any flatulence problem during school time.

Maria and the family may have been unwittingly strengthening Houla's behaviour. Houla could exert control over her body in environments other than her home. Maria was taking responsibility for her daughter's behaviour, no doubt motivated by love for her daughter. In many of our examples, we have seen that a number of actions by parents were motivated by love, but how effective or useful these actions were would be open to discussion.

Expressing Love

Love is a key ingredient in the relationship between parent and child. Hugs, cuddles, laughs and fun are vital to the health and welfare of your child. The emotional needs of child and parent can be met by a positive sharing of warmth. Switching hats from parent to adult does not mean that the spiritual and emotional bond between parent and child has to suffer. We are human beings, not robots. Be comfortable with the thought that the expression of positive emotion is part of the relationship.

Unconditional love is reflected in our capacity to have absolute faith in the goodness of our child. This fits very comfortably with our technique of visualising a positive outcome for our children.

Managing Emotion

On occasions, the child will need to know that their behaviour has upset us. They need to understand that their actions affect other people. Living in a social world requires empathy for others. The key to developing that empathy is to choose your language carefully when expressing your own feelings. You want the child to see that their attitude and behaviour has had a negative impact upon another human being. That learning should take place.

As adults, we need to discriminate between a child's behaviour and their status as a person. The expression 'unconditional love' has been around for decades. It simply means that as a parent we will always love our child. In our adult role, however, we learn to separate the child's behaviour from our love for the child.

CASE STUDY: It's just a scratch #1

Nick was an expressive ten-year-old who had worked out a set of effective techniques for aggravating his family members. One day, he irritated his mother so much that she finally exploded and told him 'You are a rotten child. I don't know why I ever had you.'

Nick took the message to heart. He had developed a view, in his mind, that his sister was the favorite child and now it had been confirmed. Unhappy with this revelation from his mother, Nick decided upon a plan of action to punish his family. He knew that his mother was very proud of her new car. She had worked hard to save for it and she constantly told the family how proud she was of it. Nick entered the garage and got his bike. As he passed his mother's car, the bike 'accidentally' fell and scraped the side of the car, causing $700 worth of repairs to the paintwork. Mother's view of Nick was reinforced. He was bad.

Mother was justifiably irritated and angered by Nick's constant misbehaviour. The words she chose to express her anger reflected the angry parent within her. The outcome was revenge on Nick's part and more trauma for everyone. Had Mother recognised and distanced herself from her feelings and expressed them in a different way, the outcome might have been different.

CASE STUDY: It's just a scratch #2

Nick was an expressive ten-year-old who had worked out a set of effective techniques for aggravating his family members. One day, he irritated his mother so much that she finally exploded and told him 'Your behaviour is totally unacceptable. I feel very angry when I see you carry on like that. When you can speak more respectfully, I'm happy to talk to you. In the meantime, I choose not to be in the same room with you.' Nick was speechless. He swore and went upstairs to his bedroom. Almost an hour later, Nick came downstairs. While he did not apologise to his Mother, his tone of voice and manner had improved. His mother noticed the improvement and chose to respond to him in a slightly cool but pleasant manner when he asked how long it would be before dinner was served.

This is not just playing with words. There will be different outcomes to situations depending the language that we choose to use. Opening your mouth and just saying it 'how it is' may be very damaging.

Choosing Our Words

Learning to use language effectively, as we saw in Chapter 6, will impact on your success. We often do not listen to what we are saying. As soon as a thought comes into our heads, we just say it without taking time to choose a better way to express it. It may be more comfortable to express ourselves in the way in which we have always done, but removing the parent hat and putting on the adult one will enable us to achieve a more effective use of language. Our child will benefit.

Consider the following conversation between a parent and child.

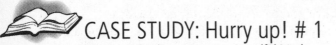

CASE STUDY: Hurry up! # 1

'How many times do I have to repeat myself?' Mother spat at Jane.

'You're always on my back,' Jane complained.

'If you don't do it now, I'm going to stop you going to Meagan's birthday party. Hurry up'.

'In a minute,' Jane replied.

'Don't give me lip, girl. Do it now!' Mother exploded.

'Shut up!' Jane retorted.

'That's it, don't think you're going to the party, you uncooperative little bitch. Don't you speak to me like that!' Mother yelled.

Jane ran out of the room in tears and slammed the door behind her.

Here is another take on the same situation.

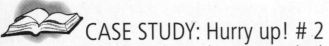

CASE STUDY: Hurry up! # 2

'Jane, I've asked you to hurry up because we are already late. If you choose to continue messing around you are also choosing not to go Meagan's party, as I won't have time to drive you. What do you want to do? We need to be out of here in five minutes.' Mother said firmly.

'Coming. I just need my CD,' Jane replied.

'You make your choice. I am not going to repeat myself.'

Mother waited. Within three minutes, Jane was at the front door, ready to go.

Carefully consider the differences. In the first conversation, Mother:
- starts the conversation by displaying her anger and impatience at Jane
- repeats her request to be ready (a sure way to teach Jane not to listen until something has been said more than once!)
- accuses Jane of not listening, which triggers a resentful response from Jane
- builds up the negative emotion in the conversation and puts her daughter down

- threatens Jane with a punishment
- achieves an outcome that is the opposite of what she originally wanted
- is into power. She believes that Jane is a puppet and that she should jump at a command issued by a parent.

In the second conversation, Mother:

- clearly and objectively states the reality of the situation
- encourages Jane to take responsibility for what she is doing and offers her a choice
- uses words that are not charged with emotion
- with a bit of patience, achieves the outcome that she wants.

Therein lies the difference. In both examples, Mother wanted to achieve the same goal. The words that were chosen and they way in which they were spoken clearly affected the outcome. The underlying attitude behind the words also differs. In the first example, Mother is locked into being a parent. She believes in power and having control. She does not teach Jane to make a decision or to think about her actions. She relies on threats and punishment to achieve her role as a parent. She is successful in creating resentment and anger in her relationship with her daughter.

Now imagine that Jane does not respond in the second example. What should happen?

CASE STUDY: Hurry up! # 3

'Jane, I've asked you to hurry up because we are already late. If you choose to continue messing around you are also choosing not to go to Meagan's party, as I won't have time to drive you. What do you want to do? We need to be out of here in five minutes.' Mother firmly asked.

'Coming, I just need my CD,' Jane replied.

'You make your choice. I am not going to repeat myself.'

Mother waited. Seven minutes later, Jane was at the front door, ready to go.

'Jane, you have chosen to take seven minutes to get ready. I clearly told you that we needed to leave within five minutes. Guess what you've chosen to do?'

'What?' asked Jane.

'Guess,' replied Mother.

'That's right – punish me!' Jane spat at her mother.

' No. I will tell you a secret. You chose not to be ready. You haven't allowed time for me to drive you to Meagan's house. So you've chosen not to go.'

Jane burst into tears.

'You can cry if you want. Just remember – you chose not to cooperate, not me,' Mother stated calmly, taking deep breaths as she did so.

Mother, as the adult, used the experience to teach Jane about consequences. Notice that she chose not to react to Jane's emotional outburst. She remained focused on using the experience to help Jane learn the connection between her behaviour and the outcome. It is probably taking more time than Mother would like to spend but it is time well invested. Jane is being well trained to become a responsible adult.

Words Can Energise

An additional benefit of developing an awareness of the words we use is that we can motivate and energise our children with greater effectiveness.

Parents are fond of the words:

- No
- Try
- Don't

Adults use these words very sparingly or eliminate them from their vocabulary.

 CASE STUDY: 'Try harder' means doing less

Richard would always make excuses for his performance in the school athletics team. He was a talented athlete but never seemed to perform to the expectation of himself, his parents or his coach.

'You have to try harder,' exhorted his coach. Richard did try. Instead of improving, he became more anxious and unsure and started to run more poorly.

'Well I've tried,' Richard admitted to his therapist. 'Nothing's improved. I'm going to give away running and take up swimming.'

'If you're going to do that,' his father responded. 'You'll have to try harder than you did at athletics.'

Richard's performance was sabotaged before he had jumped into the pool.

The difficulty with the word 'try' is that anything that follows the word is rendered passive. If, like Richard, you 'try to run better', then all the action is focused on 'try', and 'to run' becomes passive. The mind directs all its attention to trying rather than running. There is unlikely to be any improvement in the running, except by chance.

How often we exhort our children to try. We would be better able to motivate and energise our children by talking about the action.

CASE STUDY: Do it

Martin was nervous about his forthcoming exams. His goal was firmly fixed on achieving the score he needed to enter aeronautical engineering at university. This would require an excellent exam performance. Despite being a conscientious and effective student, Martin became increasingly anxious.

Martin's parents, Katrina and Frank, were very aware of his decreasing confidence. What could they do? As parents, they knew that the only role they could play was to be encouraging and supportive. It was Martin's choice to aim so high. He had to take ownership of that goal. They avoided placing their expectations on him as they were aware that parental expectations can create stress for students doing exams. They were also very conscious that telling Martin to 'try your best' or 'don't get stressed' was not likely to assist him in his quest for the best performance.

Katrina and Frank loved their son dearly and were very supportive of his goals. With great thoughtfulness, they considered how best to motivate him. In a timely, gentle and reassuring way, they would offer Martin such comments as:

'Do your best. That is all you can ask of yourself.'

'Have faith in your ability and hard work.'

'Be proud of your attitude.'

'Take the pressure off yourself, there will be a positive outcome.'

Whenever Martin initiated a conversation about his study or how he felt, they avoided nagging or asking questions about his revision.

Martin sat for his exams and was relieved to find, on receiving his final results, that he had just made the quota for aeronautical engineering. His goal had been achieved. In discussing his success, he commented about his parents that 'They were always encouraging and never put me under pressure.'

Katrina and Frank had performed well!

Chapter **8**
Conclusion

Self Assessment: Are You On the Right Track?

Take a few moments and reflect on what you have learned by reading this book. You might like to check your understanding of the key concepts by trying this checklist. The answers are on the following pages.

True or False?

1 Having children changes your life.

2 Thinking of myself as a parent is a useful way to bring up children.

3 Using techniques for being more effective in bringing up children means that I have to compromise my set of values.

4 Thinking of myself as a parent can cause me to feel pressure and lack confidence.

5 Over-parenting hinders a child's development.

6 Under-parenting can create a child who doesn't see the consequences of their behaviour.

7 Parents are into power.

8 Adults are into teaching children appropriate behaviour.

9 Parents can force their children to change.

10 The ability to make a decision is a key skill that a parent can teach to a child.

11 Adults earn respect; parents expect respect automatically.

12 Parents who think like adults negotiate with their children.

13 Peer-group pressure is the cause of most teenage problems.

14 Children learn better if you discipline them.

15 Giving a child boundaries increases their sense of security.

16 Children don't learn from failure. Parents should prevent their children from failing.

17 Giving your child too much materially can rob them of motivation.

18 Spending time with children is a key ingredient in their mental health.

19 Parents usually talk too much.

20 Reminding a child to do things does no harm.

21 Parents who are united in their approach to dealing with their children tend to do better.

22 Intervening in fights between siblings is important.

23 Shouting at a child helps them to respond to what you are saying.

24 Saying sorry to a child is a stupid thing to do because you lose their respect.

25 Language is one of the most powerful tools in parenting.

Self-Assessment: Feedback

1	True	Having children does change your life. As an adult, recognise and appropriately respond to the changes.
2	False	Locking yourself into a parent role and thinking like a parent can create difficulties. You are more likely to be an effective parent by thinking and acting as an adult.
3	False	Your values are critical to your capacity to live life.
4	True	Many parents have suffered stress from the burden of responsibility that they feel.
5	True	Over-parenting smothers a child and stunts their emotional growth and maturity.
6	True	Under-parenting leaves a child feeling insecure and poorly trained in predicting outcomes and accepting responsibility for their own behaviour.

| 7 | True | Parents believe that because the child is younger and less experienced, they are right, and have the power, to make the child conform to their rules. |

7   True   Parents believe that because the child is younger and less experienced, they are right, and have the power, to make the child conform to their rules.

8   True   Parents who think like adults appreciate the value of teaching their child appropriate behaviour.

9   True/False   Parents can coerce their child to comply with them through the use of force and punishment, but a long-term change in behaviour is less likely to occur because the child may become resentful and seek revenge.

10   True   A developed capacity to make appropriate decisions is a key to successful living.

11   True   Adults don't focus on the issue of respect. They accept their role and relationship with the child, and expect that the respect they accord their child will be automatically be returned.

12   True   Negotiation is not a threat to an adult, but it is to parents who are scared that it will mean they lose power.

13   False   Peer pressure is a myth. Under-confident children who are not trained to believe in their decision-making capabilities are prone to trying to please the group.

14   False   Children need boundaries and a clear understanding of appropriate behaviour and how to make decisions. Externally applied discipline doesn't help them to achieve skills for living.

15   True   Even teenagers like to have clear boundaries that guide them as to appropriate and inappropriate behaviour.

16   False   Successful people fail but they fail less often.

Children learn from their failures as well as their successes.

17 True   Getting too much too easily robs a child of motivation to achieve and succeed.

18 True   There is no substitute for spending time together to create a relationship.

19 True   May they learn to be quiet!

20 False   Nagging the child and constantly reminding them of things to do robs them of the opportunity to take personal responsibility.

21 True   United you stand. Divided you fall.

22 False   Intervening in fights between siblings is a great way to get your children to hate you.

23 True/False In the short term, shouting at a child will gain their attention and cooperation, but too much shouting creates an opportunity for the child to dislike you and ignore you. Would you feel positive about someone who was constantly yelling at you?

24 False   Nothing is lost by being honest. Your example in being prepared to apologise to the child makes a positive statement. It teaches the child values.

25 True   Words are powerful. Think and choose what you say carefully.

The only person you have real power to change is yourself. Your primary responsibility in life is for what you do and say. Focus on your reactions and responses to things that occur in your life. Work on those and watch the positive changes emerge.

Abandon the false belief that because you are older and a parent, you can have direct power to change someone who is younger. If you do cling to the belief that you are the parent and the child is going to do what you want or say, be prepared to embrace failure and frustration. There is no quality of life to be had from living in this way.

Alternatively, if you end up with a compliant child through fear, consider that child's capacity to lead a productive and healthy adult life. The chances of that happening are very slim.

Abandon fear. Be confident that you have worthwhile values and utilise the gift of humour in communicating with them.

Take time to think through these suggested ingredients. Discuss them with your partner if you have one, and perhaps re-read this book at some future time. Decide whether you can use them as part of your recipe for a happier family and children. Remember, too, that other areas of your life, such as work, will improve as well.

Life is not about arguments, conflict and domestic terror. Nor is it about feeling shredded and losing confidence in yourself. You did not choose to have children so that you could suffer, unless you are a masochist!

As an adult and a teacher you have the capacity to love and develop your child in healthy and creative ways. So renew your spirits, reassess your approach, take control of yourself and enjoy your role in one of the most exciting projects life can offer: the growth and development of a child.

Postscript

If you have reached this part of the book and you need extra motivation to change, let me leave you with a final thought:

As you get older, you will become childlike yourself, and your children will assume a parenting role. Do yourself a favour and invest in a happier old age. Children have long memories!

Having taught them, by example, to make appropriate decisions, you may ensure a more comfortable existence for you as a geriatric person – after all, the strongest motivation for all humans is self-interest!

Where Can I Get Help?

If you would like to talk about your child and your parenting skills with a professional, you can obtain a referral to a registered psychologist.

In Australia, you can contact the Australian Psychological Society by calling their toll free number, **1 800 333 497**, or e-mailing a request to *refer-ral@psychsociety.com.au*. This is a free referral service provided to the public by the Australian Psychological Society, and covers metropolitan and rural areas throughout Australia.

In United States and Canada, you can find a psychologist by going to www.findapsychologist.org. The American Psychological Association's online Help Center (www.apahelpcenter.org) also features helpful resources and a 'Find a Psychologist' database.

In the United Kingdom, psychologists can be found by clicking on the 'Find a Psychologist' link on the British Psychological Society's website (www. bps.org.uk).

In New Zealand, the New Zealand Psychological Society's website (www. psychology.org.nz) can direct you to a database of local psychologists.

Bibliography

Over the decades, I have seen all manner of parenting courses, theories and books come, go and in some cases stay. Each of the following books will stimulate your thinking.

Balson, Maurice, *Becoming Better Parents*, 4th edn, ACER, Camberwell, Vic., 1994

Biddulph, Stephen, *The Secret of Happy Children*, HarperCollinsPublishers, Sydney, 1998

Cheetham, John et al, *Back on Track! Stress Reducing Strategies* (double CD), Wilkins Farago, Melbourne, 2005

Covey, Stephen, *Daily Reflections for Highly Effective People*, The Business Library, Melbourne, 1994

De Vries, Peter, *The Tunnel of Love*, Little, Brown and Company, New York, 1954

DeBono, Edward, *Teach Your Child How to Think*, Penguin, London, 1993

Goleman, Daniel, *Emotional Intelligence*, Bloomsbury Publishing, London, 1996

Gyatso, Tenzin (the Fourteenth Dalai Lama of Tibet), *Ancient Wisdom, Modern World*, Little, Brown and Company, London, 1999

Whatham, Mick, *Days of Yore*, Days of Yore Publishers, Kerang, Vic., 2000

Fuller, Andrew, *Raising Real People*, ACER, Camberwell, Vic., 2000

Your feedback or enquiry is welcome!

You can contact the author at PO Box 478, Cheltenham 3192, Australia, or by email at **growup.johncheetham@ gmail.com**

Further information about the Student Achievement Centre can be found at:

www.studentachievement.com.au

Also available: Back on Track CD

Torn between the demands of work and home? Never have time for yourself? Worried about your relationships? Arguing with the kids? Feeling constantly pressured? Sick of living with stress?

Featuring John Cheetham and other Australian psychologists, this double audio CD is the way to get yourself back on track.

Back on Track! Stress Reducing Strategies
ISBN 9780975700204, $36.95 (2-CD)
Order through your local bookshop or **www.wilkinsfarago.com.au**